The Pattern of our Calling

The Pattern of our Calling

Ministry yesterday, today and tomorrow

David Hoyle

scm press

© David Hoyle 2016

Published in 2016 by SCM Press
Editorial office
3rd Floor, Invicta House,
108–114 Golden Lane,
London EC1Y 0TG, UK

Hymns Ancient & Modern® is a registered trademark
of Hymns Ancient and Modern Ltd

SCM Press is an imprint of Hymns Ancient & Modern Ltd
(a registered charity)
13A Hellesdon Park Road, Norwich,
Norfolk NR6 5DR, UK

www.scmpress.co.uk

Scripture quotations are from the New Revised Standard Version of
the Bible, Anglicized Edition, copyright © 1989, 1995 by the Division
of Christian Education of the National Council of the Churches of
Christ in the USA. Used by permission. All rights reserved.

British Library Cataloguing in Publication data

A catalogue record for this book is available
from the British Library

978 0 334 05472 6

Typeset by Regent Typesetting
Printed and bound by
CPI Group (UK) Ltd

Contents

Preface   ix
Abbreviations   xiii

 1 Beginning Badly   1
 2 Through Confusions   10
 3 Tasks in Ministry   19
 4 Outreaching Speech   36
 5 Putting Priests in Their Place   59
 6 Ministers of the Kingdom   88
 7 Holiness   100
 8 Gifts in Ministry   132
 9 Keeping Your Balance   153
10 Spiritual Traffic   175

Index of Biblical References   189
Index of Names   190

v

For Michael Perham
and for the ministers,
lay and ordained,
in the Dioceses of Gloucester and Bristol,
with thanks

Preface

An email arrived; she was back from a funeral. 'It was for an old family friend,' she wrote, 'and it was a good "do" – apart from the sermon, which was rather grandstanding and "all about me" rather than "all about our friend who had died". That *really* annoys me!' It is one of the ways that ministry goes wrong. In fact, it is one of the ways ministry most often goes wrong, it gets in the way, we cannot see past the person or the performance. The important point about ministry is that it is so often done so selflessly and so well, but sometimes it does go wrong. Ministry goes wrong in other ways. It can be overbearing and officious; too noisy, or too quiet; it can be gossipy and unkind; it can be divisive; and it can be indecisive. Now and again it becomes just downright peculiar, or a bit weird.

We notice when ministry goes wrong and we don't need any kind of expertise to do so. Like a musical instrument that has not been properly tuned, when we get it wrong the sheer wrongness of it tugs at our attention. We can agree where ministry has gone wrong. We do not find it nearly so easy to agree about what we look for instead. We want the clergy to point away from themselves, and it is a slightly tricky business describing just how you do that. In the pages that follow, you will find some of the things we have said about ministry over the years. You cannot help but notice that we have said a number of different things. It seems that we can agree that it is important and that it might go wrong and, after that, we start saying very different things.

While ministry has never been precisely defined, there have been times when we have been more or less in agreement about what we expect and times when we are less so. This is one of the moments when we are arguing the point. We are less sure we agree and, of course because we are less sure, we are more opinionated and a little more strident. So, ministry is contested and the very thing that we depend upon to unite the Church becomes one of the things that divides it. There will never be a last word on ministry; we will never reach that elusive definition. One of the things that we are reminded of whenever we begin a ministry, and make the Declaration of Assent, is that this is for a reason: 'Bringing the grace and truth of Christ to this generation.' So, if you read your way to the end of the book and wonder if I am offering some sort of answer, I am not. I do think we have forgotten where we are supposed to go for advice, and I know this is a conversation that will never be finished.

This is not a history of ministry and it is certainly not an exhaustive survey of the books about ministry. This is just one more contribution to that conversation about ministry. As we try to bring the grace and truth of Christ to this generation, here is some background reading.

Because ministry is contested at the moment it might be best to acknowledge there are assumptions here that you may, or may not, like. This is, largely, a book about ordained ministry. Read it and I hope you will see that I really do know that ministry belongs to the whole people of God. I happen to be a priest, however, and it is the conversation about ministerial priesthood that is contested, so this is, largely, a book about priests. There is also a problem about language. A lot of the authors mentioned in this book wrote at a time when women were not ordained, and their language is exclusively male. I believe that ministry belongs to women and men, and where I can be inclusive I have been, but I have not altered the texts I cite.

The book comes out of Gloucester and Bristol, but the first draft was written in Magdalene College, Cambridge, during some study leave. The Bishop of Gloucester and my colleagues in the Department of Ministry made it possible for me to go there, and the Master and Fellows of Magdalene made me welcome. I am deeply grateful to them all. I have been supported with kindness and consideration and offered encouragement at every turn. David Shervington, Hannah Ward and those who work with them at SCM Press have been patient, wise and immensely helpful. Colleagues in Bristol Cathedral not only made it possible for me to finish the job, they did that without once making me feel that I was imposing on them, when I clearly was. Particular thanks go to Eamon Duffy and Stephen Hampton, who suggested books I should read. Christopher Bryan, Wendy Burton, Tom Clammer, Kathy Lawrence, Martyn Percy and John Witcombe read parts of the book in draft and helped me avoid some bad mistakes. The errors that remain are all my own work.

My family were endlessly long-suffering with the slow business of writing. Without the confidence they gave me this book would never have been finished. In a sense it is their book, but it is dedicated to all those with whom I shared the ministry of God, in the Dioceses of Gloucester and Bristol, bishops, clergy and laity. When I have tried to teach them, I have learnt from them and, when I tried to help them, they helped me more than they will ever know.

DMH

Abbreviations

ANF   A. Roberts and J. Donaldson (eds), *Ante-Nicene Fathers*, Peabody MA: Hendrickson Publishing, 1999.

N&PNF 1S   P. Schaff (ed.), *Nicene and Post-Nicene Fathers, First Series*, Peabody MA: Hendrickson Publishing, 1999.

N&PNF 2S   P. Schaff and H. Wace (eds), *Nicene and Post-Nicene Fathers, Second Series*, Peabody MA: Hendrickson Publishing, 1999.

God has given particular ministries. Priests are ordained to lead God's people in the offering of praise and the proclamation of the gospel. They share with the Bishop in the oversight of the Church, delighting in its beauty and rejoicing in its well-being. They are to set the example of the Good Shepherd always before them as the pattern of their calling.

From the Bishop's Introduction to the
Ordination of Priests, Common Worship
copyright © The Archbishops' Council 2007

I

Beginning Badly

There are, I know, plenty of other stories just like this one. This particular story is neither unusual, nor startling. It is, though, my story. It is where I make my beginning.

It was a June night, 30 years ago, and some of the details are a bit hazy now. I cannot even remember after all this time precisely what it was that he said. Perhaps that does not matter very much because the story is, after all, so familiar. In fact, I don't suppose he said a great deal. He was a shy and scholarly man; words were chosen carefully; they never came in a rush. There were always half hesitations and little silences in his company. In fact, it was precisely because he was so reticent that the gesture he made was so remarkable and made such a difference. It was a very little thing that he did, but that night it steered me through a little crisis, and I am still grateful all these years later.

I was in charge of books and candles and so on. I don't suppose anyone had actually asked me to do that. I had a bustling, chipper enthusiasm and was always inventing jobs that may, or may not, have needed doing. So, because I had to see to the candles and the lights, I was on my feet as the service ended and I was first out of the chapel. First out of the chapel, behind the bishop, and so he could not fail to see that all my absurd enthusiasm and busy confidence had suddenly quite drained away.

It was the last night of the ordination retreat. With the others, who were still sitting over their prayers in the chapel, I was due in the cathedral the following morning, to be ordained deacon. Like so very many men and women, before and since, I was suddenly swept with great tides of doubt and fear. Ordination retreats usually close with a bishop's 'charge'. For several days, a retreat conductor leads those to be ordained through a period of quiet preparation. At the end of the retreat, there is a change of gear and the bishop, who will soon ordain in the name of Christ and his Church, speaks words of encouragement, instruction or challenge. Gathering for the bishop's charge everyone knows they have come to a threshold and everyone feels the significance of the moment. Most of our bishops, sensibly, do not tug on the heartstrings. Well aware that they are speaking to men and women who are on a roller coaster of anxiety and excitement, they speak calmly of important truths.

Earlier generations did things differently. In Durham, in the 1880s, J. B. Lightfoot could not resist ramming the point home. This was a defining moment, a time for decisions:

> A great change in your lives, a tremendous pledge given, a tremendous responsibility incurred, a magnificent blessing claimed, a glorious potentiality of good bestowed – how else shall I describe the crisis which to-morrow's sun will bring, or at least may bring to all of you ...
>
> A great and momentous change – momentous beyond all human conception for good and evil, to yourselves, to your flock, to every one who comes in contact with you. For good or for evil. It must be so. This is the universal law in things spiritual. The same Christ, Who is for the rising of many, is for the falling of many likewise. The same gospel, which is to some the savour of life unto life, is to others the savour of death unto death. A potentiality of glory must likewise be a potentiality of shame.[1]

Earlier generations, notice, knew the risk, knew the possibilities of failure and success.

In Ely in 1986, we did not get anything like that from the bishop. I would have bolted if I had heard anything like that. I was all in a mood for bolting. The retreat had already provided more than enough in the way of defining moments. It had been led by W. H. Vanstone, a man who had digested his own experience of an acutely uncomfortable parish ministry and brilliantly laid it bare in the book *Love's Endeavour, Love's Expense*. Vanstone had been a taciturn, intense presence throughout the retreat. Self-contained and understated, he was nonetheless a man of passionate conviction and it all got distilled into a series of addresses about ordained ministry lived and worked 'out on the boundaries'. Vanstone had learnt, at great personal cost, what kind of work a priest can do with people who are struggling to negotiate something at the very borders of their experience: in sickness, bereavement or anxiety. A priest who is going to be any use in conversations like that, he told us, has to be out on those same boundaries too and know just how uncomfortable that can feel. Priests are called to the boundaries, he said, and to the knowledge that there our capacity and resources would be stretched to the limit. I took the point, but there was a cold fear in me. So, by the final night of the retreat, I was seriously thinking of bolting.

In his charge, the Bishop of Ely talked a little about Dietrich Bonhoeffer and about the poet Geoffrey Hill. Arrested by the Nazis in 1943, the Lutheran pastor Dietrich Bonhoeffer spent his first Christmas in captivity watching the flares falling from allied bombers over Berlin. Geoffrey Hill's poem *Christmas Trees* places Bonhoeffer between two types of violence, between the Nazi state that imprisoned him, and the violence of flares and bombs falling from the sky. In *Letters and Papers from Prison*, Bonhoeffer wrestled with the problem of what theology and the Church should say in times as bad as that. He favoured restraint over passion: 'Qualified silence might perhaps be more appropriate for the Church today than very unqualified speech.'[2] So, Geoffrey Hill describes the measured discipline of Bonhoeffer gently insisting we must hear sounds nearly drowned out by horror. He has him speak words that 'are quiet but not too quiet'.[3]

'His words are quiet, but not too quiet.' My bishop might have been sparing with words, and gentle in manner, but it was not because he had nothing to say. There was nothing uncertain or confused about him. He was a man rich in learning, full of reference, and even the silences had a kind of authority; he was, himself, precisely 'quiet, but not too quiet'. He pointed us towards a ministry that would first hear the truth and then speak it.

I did not for a moment disagree, but I was by now mentally packing my bags and planning my great escape. These were demands I could not meet. And so he saw me, as I left the chapel, frightened of running away and frightened of staying. That seriously shy man put his arm round my shoulders and propelled me into the garden where we walked up and down in near darkness for 15 minutes. Initially, of course, he just had hold of me and I wasn't going anywhere, except where he was going. Later, I knew I had to stay. I had to stay because I was suddenly in company; I walked in that garden, at night, with someone else. Ministry was not and never would be something I did alone. I had, at last, also been reminded that ordination really was not simply a test of my talents and my convictions. I was being ordained, by a bishop, into the Church of God. Properly understood, ordination might indeed set me apart and despatch me to those boundaries I feared, but it would also always remind me that I would be included in something, swept up in the great purposes of God. The work that worried me so much would never really be mine.

Ministry belongs to the Church. At ordination we are told that 'The Church is the Body of Christ, the people of God and the dwelling place of the Holy Spirit.' Ministry is modelled by Christ then shared in that community. Ministry is never a possession; it is always an inheritance. The fundamental character of ministry is its relatedness to the ministry of the whole people of God. Richard Baxter, a Nonconformist minister writing in the seventeenth century made the point that so many others have made:

> By your work you are related to Christ, as well as to the flock. You are stewards of his mysteries, and rulers of his household; and he that entrusted you, will maintain you in his work ... Be true to him and never doubt that he will be true to you.[4]

Lightfoot made a similar point; he talked about ordinands who make two errors. First, they get anxious about whether or not the work is going well, instead of just doing the work because it is important and serves God. Then they get self-conscious and wonder if they can do it at all. Like Jeremiah, they find themselves saying, 'I cannot speak: for I am a child.'

> As well dash my head against a fortress of stone, as attempt so hopeless a task. What can I do to heal this wounded spirit, to melt this hardened conscience, to soothe these dying agonies? Who am I, that I should act as Christ's ambassador, should bear God's message to these? I am tongue-tied. I can only stammer, can only lisp out half-formed words like a child?
>
> And the reproof comes to you as it came to Jeremiah of old, 'Say not, I am a child. Be not afraid of their faces.' And the promise is vouchsafed to you now, as it was vouchsafed to him then, 'I am with thee to deliver thee.' 'Behold I have put My words in thy mouth.'[5]

Ministry is not something we own, it comes from Christ. It is his work before it is ours.

That night, walking round and round the little lawn, I began to understand this better. I knew I had to stay. I did not really understand it then, but I would soon begin to see that a vocation is not a choice you make and certainly not a commitment to excel. I don't think the bishop believed in my abilities, I doubt if he even believed in the miraculous power of the ordination rite, but he believed in my vocation. He believed I was called by Christ and that if I was true to him, he would be true to me.

So, my ordained ministry began with some serious questions about what on earth I thought I was doing. Strangely, that crisis passed and never returned. I have had dreadful days and, at one stage, months and months when I have wondered what to do next and berated myself for my failure to live up to my calling. There have been real crises because I have been wrong and because I have done things badly. The question about whether I should be doing it *at all* has, however, never returned. I have been very lucky. Others around me, including at one stage a close colleague, have been dogged again and again by that particular, cruel uncertainty. It takes all sorts of forms. That night in Ely, I faced a question about my own vocation because I had been labouring with the dreadful, cocky conceit that ministry was going to be a test of my abilities and a public performance. That brought me to a crisis of confidence and courage. Now I am (slightly) less fascinated with my own reflection. The temptation to assume this must all be about me has passed. Still, it was there, in that night in the garden of a retreat house that this book, about ministry and priesthood, had its beginning.

Having resisted the dreadful temptation to bolt, I served a (rather short) curacy on a modern housing estate, and then went on to be a college chaplain. For seven years I taught history to undergraduates, took chapel services in term time, and let bursars and clerks of works worry about bills and maintenance. I worked as a pastor in a small community where I knew nearly everyone by name and where I knew and felt all the rhythms of the student year. It was all very exciting, and energetic, and opinionated, and I loved it, but it wasn't a preparation for parish ministry.

After seven years of college, and claret, and conversation, I was instituted and inducted as a vicar and discovered I had no map for the journey. At first, of course, I simply did not know the place or the people, and struggled with a fairly hefty culture shock. That was hard, but the real problem was something more fundamental and more destructive than that. My difficulty was that I had no real idea of what a priest was supposed to do, or be. I worked hard, but usually felt I was doing the wrong thing or (just as uncomfortable) the right thing badly. The poor parishioners I went to work among needed endless patience as I lurched from anxious inactivity into frantic, misplaced effort. Fortunately, they proved to have patience by the bucket load. So, the question was slowly refined. I was no longer so concerned to know how best to use my gifts as a priest; I was much more concerned to know what a priest was, what a priest did.

When I moved again that question began to loom very large indeed. I became a member of the new legion of diocesan officials, responsible for ministry. I had been a vicar, now I became an 'officer' and, a bit later, a 'director'. The titles bother me a bit. If you need an 'officer for ministry' there might be an implication that ministry is *official* and needs organizing from an office. The business of being a 'director' is even more disturbing, partly because of all those pinstripe associations in the boardroom, and partly because of the implication that ministry might need a diocesan official to give it *direction*. That is a simply ludicrous idea. It is ludicrous because ministry is local and happens in particular places, among particular people, and does not readily lend itself to direction from outside. It is also ludicrous because we are virtually all agreed that ministry is changing fast and being done in all kinds of different ways. There is simply not enough agreement among us for us easily to accept direction from someone with an office and a computer and a few books. There is a variety of practice and opinion that is pulling us apart. Like it or not though (and, in truth, it was a job I loved), I had become a director of ministry and I was supposed to have something to say about what ministry is.

I left that job six years ago and among the boxes and bits and pieces that were carried from my house when we moved was a first draft of this book. Now I am a dean and my experience of ministry has changed again. One of my current jobs is to keep 'open house' for the diocese. A cathedral is the theatre for diocesan relationships. A dean can make those relationships easier, or more difficult. What I see, in the cathedral, suggests to me that our conversations are more problematic than they used to be. The clergy are stretched thinly and work with ordained colleagues less and less often. We are less collegiate, and cathedrals, staffed by a dean and canons, look privileged. Cathedrals are also beginning to look odd. The worship of the Church of England is more various than it has ever been. Choral evensong, which was once the benchmark for Anglican practice, is now unfamiliar territory. At the end of a service that I had thoroughly enjoyed, a fairly senior parish priest cornered me and jabbed me with a finger: 'What had that got to do with the price of fish?' The truth is that the clergy can no longer summon up a common culture, and a common practice becomes more difficult. Our meetings become clumsier.

So, this book is written to answer questions about ministry that I have asked myself over and again. It is written too out of the more recent experience of talking to others who ask similar questions. There are dozens and dozens of books about ministry. I have read quite a lot of them and discuss a few in the pages that follow. The Church now echoes with the sound of the clergy talking to themselves, about themselves. I feel more than a bit shifty about adding my voice to that din. There is, though, something I want to say. Since that night in Ely, I have been interested in the question, 'What are priests supposed to do?' I believe that same question is now being posed with mounting urgency and a fresh impatience. We have passed through a period when we have debated our calling and sat loose to any one solution. Now, a church eager to be more effective in mission and more anxious than ever about its future is suddenly discovering a new determination to insist that ministry should look and sound like focused leadership with clear strategic goals. Not so long ago we struggled because ministry was various and we scattered in different directions. Now we are struggling because some of us are very clear that we know exactly what ministry should be doing and some of us do not like the direction of travel.

Ministry is an inheritance, not a possession. The language we are using is new. It needs testing. This new vocabulary is sometimes accompanied by an insistence that old ideas and old practices have constrained us and even compromised our work. Here, I want to ask if that is so. What helped me that night as I stood at the beginning of something new was to be reminded that I belonged in company. This book is a study of the company we keep in ministry. Others, before us, came to their own ordinations in fear and excitement and worked out the grace of orders in other places and at other times. So, alongside the new vocabulary here is the old. It is offered in the hope that it might do for someone else what once Peter, Bishop of Ely, did for me, on the night before my ordination. Here is a reminder that we are in good company and not as isolated as we might feel.

Notes

1 J. B. Lightfoot, *Ordination Addresses and Counsels to Clergy*, VI, London: Macmillan, 1890, pp. 67–8 (preached 1882, 1886).

2 D. Bonhoeffer, *No Rusty Swords*, trans. E. Robertson and J. Bowden, New York: Harper & Row, 1965, p. 160.

3 G. Hill, *Collected Poems*, London: Viking Press, 1985, p. 73.

4 R. Baxter, *The Reformed Pastor*, Chapter 2, section 3.1.5, Edinburgh: Banner of Truth, 1974, p. 128.

5 Lightfoot, *Ordination Addresses*, I, pp. 10–11.

2

Through Confusions

In the basement of a Cambridge bookshop, years ago, two clergymen were hunting for bargains among the remaindered books. They got the measure of one another with sly glances; another dog collar, another grey tweed jacket, and the mutual search for something more among the piles of dated commentaries. Then they reached for the same book and all that cautious reserve had to be abandoned. They introduced themselves. They were both vicars in Cambridgeshire villages, miles apart. Their conversation went something like this. 'Good Morning,' said one, 'I'm the Vicar of Over, with Under and Seething-in-the-Wake.' 'Hello,' said the other, 'I'm Dankly, and Deeper-in-the-Fen.' No names, notice; they did not introduce themselves as 'Michael', or 'Malcolm'. Instead, they exchanged titles and places. They introduced themselves by reference to what they did and where they did it.

This book is about priests and what priests do. There are, already, a lot of books about priests, many of them written recently. We are awash with opinion. That is because we are worried about the Church and we think ministry might be the problem and certainly needs to be the solution. A post-war generation of clergy worked to familiar routines. Then, in the years after the *Tiller Report*, those assumptions began to look less and less sure.[1] Our theology started to sound provisional and our ideas about parishes and the work of lay and ordained ministers sounded like a work in progress. In 2001 the Church of England's publishers gave us *Ministry Issues*, a major study of the ministry of the Church of England. It was a brand new and topical book as I began work as an officer for ministry. Edited by Gordon Kuhrt, who was then Director of Ministry for the Church of England, it was an authoritative survey. In his Preface, however, there was a careful disclaimer: 'This report is more like a building site than a completed and decorated monument. It offers a series of pictures and snapshots of ministry issues, many of which are moving and changing.'[2]

Four years later, another book, *The Vicar's Guide*, began with a chapter called 'The Changing Role of the Vicar' and seemed to promise that things would only get more confusing. Looking into the future, Guy Wilkinson imagined ministries becoming 'more varied, less secure and more open-ended'.[3] Ministry was in transition and people who wrote about ministry talked about change. Meanwhile, Robin Greenwood urged us to shake off tired and damaging assumptions; Steven Croft suggested we could rediscover biblical models that would help us adapt; and Chris Edmondson advised us to take care of ourselves as we went out into this storm.[4]

There are all kinds of reasons why we are feeling uncertain, and experiencing what Wilkinson called 'provisionality'.[5] Falling church attendance and financial constraint have changed us. We do things differently now. We have to do things differently now. Clergy were once fundamentally associated with a place. The two priests in the Cambridge bookshop exchanged place names by way of introduction. The assumption that we are placed by parish has shaped us for hundreds of years. In 1808, Francis Witts succeeded his uncle, the splendidly named Ferdinando Tracy Travell, as Rector of Upper Slaughter. Six years later he added the benefice of Stanway (where there had been a family home) to his responsibilities (and appointed a curate to do the work). When he died, in 1854, he was succeeded, as Rector, by his own son and later by his grandson. That is what continuity once looked like. In 2015 a new priest was appointed as Rector of Upper Slaughter. She does not live in Witts' grand rectory (that is now an elegant hotel). Nor will she focus her ministry on the one parish. She is licensed to the benefice of Guiting Power with Farmcote, Upper and Lower Slaughter, Naunton, Temple Guiting with Cutsdean and Eyford, and she also serves as Area Dean. Her impressive ministry is stretched over villages that she will struggle to know intimately, places where men, women and children leap in and out of cars to spend their weekdays in London, Cheltenham or Oxford. In rural England the vicar is now very rarely seen on a bicycle or strolling down the street. She will be in a car flailing between villages, the boot full of different hymn books for different churches, a large bottle of water for the font in one church, a blanket for another (because there is no power supply), and a CD player for a third, where there is electricity but no organist. The vicar is no longer known or recognized, as Witts would have been known and recognized. I was a parish priest for seven years in a fairly prosperous North London suburb. Walking home one day, in sight of the imposing parish church, I passed a young woman and overheard her say to her partner, 'O look, there's a vicar out walking.' I wasn't just unfamiliar, I had become a curiosity.

Relationship to the place has changed and so too has the way the clergy relate to us. It is now well over 30 years since Anthony Russell wrote his book, *The Clerical Profession*, and identified a seismic shift in the way we think about the work and role of a priest. Francis Witts took his ministry seriously, but it is not clear from his diary that his priesthood was what defined him. He lived the life of a gentleman; his relationships and his social life were shaped by his class and his wealth as much as by his ordination vows. He never went to theological college (they had not been invented in 1808, when he was ordained) and he had never heard of General Synod, Continuing Ministerial Education, Clergy Terms of Service, Child Protection, the *Guidelines for the Professional Conduct of the Clergy*, or the Archbishops' Council.

Clergy who have been used to talking about ministry as more a matter of 'being' than of 'doing' are now adapting to the lessons of performance management that other professions learnt years ago. High time too, but we have to notice that it is not just behaviour that has changed. Relationships have altered. Priests have been given intimate access to people's lives; they have heard confidences and they have been expected to speak wisely about problems that have divided families and shattered hope. Priests have been invited into uncharted

territory and they have gone there. When Wesley Carr and
W. H. Vanstone wrote the books that shaped my early years
in ministry they wrote precisely about making a commitment
to something risky and ill-defined. Now we are clearer about
the need for accountability, we talk about *professional conduct*
and *professional good practice*. The problem for the clergy is
that professionals engage with us contractually; they do this
and not that, we require of them certain skills. Professional
relationships have defined boundaries. What was unspoken
must now be agreed, and what was open-ended must have constraints. So, there are losses, as well as gains, as we become
professional. More worryingly, we have taken this step rather
late in the day. We are adopting professional attitudes just at
the point when the high culture of the professions is being criticized as elitist and even pompous. We have cloaked ourselves
in this new respectability and process and find we are being
asked instead about our character and commitment.

Facing challenging circumstances and a changing society,
ministry has altered and adapted, but adaptability is a tricky
business; it is a moving target. Ministry becomes provisional
and no one solution seems to suffice. The Church has changed
patterns of recruitment and training; it has altered and elabor-
ated forms of ministry offering us more acronyms than we
easily remember: SSMs, MSEs and OLMs. Ministry has multiplied and diversified; there is not one model, there are many;
there is not one theology, there is an academy of reflection.
There have been benefits in all this variety, and plenty of new
ministries have flourished. There has also been an unlooked-for
consequence. Put simply, we have lost our common culture.
Ministry now differs significantly from place to place. In rural
dioceses, clergy must work across parish boundaries, but in
urban centres 'one vicar – one parish' often still holds good.
There are plants and pioneers, there is 'emerging church' and
'clusters', 'hubs' and 'minsters'. We train not just in colleges,
but on courses and on 'pathways'. Our ordinands are often
older and more experienced than used to be the case. A new
parish priest might already have had a career as a nurse, a
management consultant, a merchant seaman, or an engineer.

All of it is cause for celebration (and, if we are honest, we still have a very long way to go in embracing diversity), but training institutions, deanery chapters and bishops must now work harder to create a community and association out of this variety. We talk about context more; we recognize that local experience matters. The work of a stipendiary curate on a Sheffield housing estate is not easily compared with the equally significant experience of a House for Duty priest in a village in the fens. When they meet, when we arrange training for them, the conversations are more cautious than they were and misunderstandings surface quickly.

We have grown used to breadth, diversity and permission-giving. That has been the experience of the first 30 years of my own ministry. Very recently, however, there has been another significant change of gear. There is a new agenda now and it is urgent, there is not much room for any other business. The Church of England is adopting a narrower focus, a greater emphasis on a few strategic goals and a 'simplification' programme. The language used about church and ministry has changed again. In his first Lambeth Lecture in March 2015, the Archbishop said:

> I want to start by saying just two simple sentences about the Church. First, the Church exists to worship God in Jesus Christ.
>
> Second, the Church exists to make new disciples of Jesus Christ. Everything else is decoration. Some of it may be very necessary, useful, or wonderful decoration – but it's decoration.[6]

That is a definition of Church that gives a very particular focus for ministry. The focus is mission and growth. No surprise therefore that a report on ministry (usually referred to as 'The Green Report') in September 2014 made no mention of provisionality. The Introduction to the Green Report quoted a presidential address to General Synod made by the Archbishop of Canterbury: 'we are custodians of the gospel that transforms individuals, nations and societies. We are called by God to respond radically and imaginatively to new contexts.[7] If that is the challenge, then, according to the Green Report, the business of ministry is *leadership*. It is leadership that delivers change. It is leadership that will drive mission and growth. The Green Report describes how you might identify and train future leaders.

This new emphasis on leadership is being equipped with significant resources. There is a budget for a learning community of future leaders and a significantly increased investment in training bishops and deans. This stress on leadership is rapidly becoming the *controlling* model of ministry. Focus has replaced diversity, and ministry is being invigorated with fresh and particular purpose. The Green Report is littered with phrases like 'exceptional potential', 'management capabilities' and 'sustainable capacity'. To be fair, the Green Report was never intended for publication and never pretended to be a profound theological investigation of the ministry of the Church. It is also just one wave in what is now a turning tide. Leadership was already one of the criteria that those selecting our future clergy must examine. When a diocese advertises for a new parish priest, it routinely looks for 'leadership skills'. Courses in Christian leadership abound, and books on ministry are now very often books on *leadership*.[8] Leadership becomes the name of the game.

Ministry is changing. Ministry has always changed. The conversation about the life and work of a priest changes and we notice that. There are books written that suggest that it is harder than it has ever been.[9] Sermons are preached and meetings conducted where the language is urgent and even radical. Before we throw our hands up in horror we might remind ourselves it is just different, it is not suddenly *uniquely* difficult. Good sociologists that we are, we are getting accustomed to telling one another about the complexities of the present moment. Too often, though, we are poor historians, forgetting all the shattering changes of culture and practice that we have *already* negotiated. We forget it has always been difficult. Ministry has been made and then made again. The creation of parishes, the Lateran reforms, the collapse of community in the plague years, the turmoil of reformations and Commonwealth, the Oxford Movement, the Parish Communion Movement (to name but a few) all shifted assumptions about ministry. So, for example, Eamon Duffy can describe the gale that blew through English parishes in the sixteenth century, stripping out the furniture and demolishing the framework of association. In *The Voices of Morebath* he shows us a priest reinventing himself and his ministry, not once, but again and again.[10] Elsewhere, he describes the shift of culture brought by Roman Catholic, Tridentine reform. He paints a portrait of the priest of the Middle Ages, not a spiritual figure, but 'a conscientious workman providing essential services'; he continues:

> Trent and the Counter Reformation had a different, more exalted vision. The priest was to be a man apart for the people, but, it followed, also a man apart *from* the people: his life must be conformed to the miracle he performed each day at the altar. He was to be a man of prayer, an example of personal sanctity. He was to be expert in theology and ethics, a spiritual guide to others, and the voice of a teaching *magisterium* which was ever more detailed and comprehensive in its concerns.[11]

Ministry is always a work in progress and there are plenty of books that can spell that out for us.[12] We have adapted before and we will adapt again. The interesting question is not whether we must change, but *why*. So, that question that reared up before me one night in Ely still needs an answer: 'What are priests supposed to do?'

This is not another history. There is some history here, but only as a reminder that we do actually *have* some history, that inheritance of faith. We have grown a bit impatient with history lately. I need to admit that I am a historian. I am a historian, but I am not an antiquarian; I don't want to take us back. This is not an elegy; a dying sigh offered in the conviction that the best is behind us. Christian faith is not backward-looking. We are indeed confident that God was revealed in the streets of Jerusalem and on the hills of Galilee, and seen perfectly in the cross on Golgotha. We were never meant to stay there, however. We have heard a summons to a Kingdom that lies ahead. The future is what defines us. We must not be trapped by nostalgia, nor defined by the present 'crisis'. Unless we want to resign ourselves to being rabbits in the headlights of a rushing juggernaut, we have to interrogate the assumptions we are forming. Knowing our history, knowing more than *this*, is one way to escape the crabbed confines of pressing anxiety. When urgency turns into stridency, and focus becomes impatience, mistakes are made and an argument might be lost simply because it was never had. Knowing our history, we can ask the right questions and face the future with renewed confidence. Reflecting on Christ and the pattern of our calling, we might acknowledge that we keep good company and renew our determination to proclaim the faith afresh.

Notes

1 J. Tiller, *A Strategy for the Church's Ministry*, London: CIO Publishing, 1983.

2 *Ministry Issues for the Church of England*, ed. G. W. Kuhrt, London: Church House Publishing, 2001, p. xiii.

3 G. Wilkinson, 'The Changing Role of the Vicar', in D. Ison (ed.), *The Vicar's Guide: Life and Ministry in the Parish*, London: Church House Publishing, 2005, p. 1.

4 R. Greenwood, *Parish Priests: For the Sake of the Kingdom*, London: SPCK, 2009; S. Croft, *Ministry in Three Dimensions: Ordination and Leadership in the Local Church*, London: Darton, Longman & Todd, 1999; C. Edmondson, *Fit to Lead: Sustaining Effective Ministry in a Changing World*, London: Darton, Longman & Todd, 2002.

5 Wilkinson, 'The Changing Role of the Vicar', p. 6.

6 Archbishop Justin Welby, Lambeth Lecture, 5 March 2014, http://www.archbishopofcanterbury.org/articles.php/5515/lambeth-lectures-archbishop-justin-on-evangelism-video.

7 *Talent Management for Future Leaders and Leadership Development for Bishops and Deans: A New Approach* (The Green Report), 'Introduction', p. 3, https://www.churchofengland.org/media/2130591/report.pdf.

8 There are so many of these books that Modem publishes a 'best of' list on its website, http://www.modem-uk.org/resources/MODEM+Best+21st+Century+Leadership+Books.pdf.

9 A. Clitherow, *Renewing Faith in Ordained Ministry: New Hope for Tired Clergy*, London: SPCK, 2004, pp. 9–12, 19–20; Y. Warren, *The Cracked Pot: The State of Today's Anglican Parish Clergy*, Stowmarket: Kevin Mayhew, 2002, pp. 19–30.

10 E. Duffy, *The Voices of Morebath: Reformation and Rebellion in an English Village*, New Haven, CT and London: Yale University Press, 2001.

11 E. Duffy, *Faith of Our Fathers: Reflections on Catholic Tradition*, London: Continuum, 2004, p. 106.

12 A good place to start would be M. Percy, *Clergy: The Origin of the Species*, London: Continuum, 2006.

3

Tasks in Ministry

Amateur or professional?

A few weeks into beginning a job at Gloucester Cathedral, and 'in residence' for the first time as a canon, I was summoned from what I was doing because a visitor wanted to see me. The visitor turned out to be from the BBC and she had arrived to make a programme about the cathedral. She had a clipboard, a briefcase and a timetable. She looked at her watch at regular intervals. She was also, frankly, disappointed that I wasn't the dean. She was fairly clear that it was the dean she needed to talk to. She asked me, 'What do you do here?' and, like generations of clergy before me, I struggled to find the telling phrase that summed up just exactly what it was I 'did'. My difficulty puzzled her. She knew what she did, she made television programmes. Why couldn't I explain myself as simply?

Despite the fact that I had a new deed of appointment and a job description, I struggled. I struggled because it is hard to explain how cathedrals work in just a few words (actually, cathedrals never work in a few words, but that is another story). There was, however, another part to my dilemma that morning, when I was asked to account for myself. My particular job was not only new to me, but a relatively recent departure. I had been appointed 'Director of Ministry' and there were questions to answer about how and what I directed.

For good reason we are learning to hold ourselves to account. We have terms of service, statements of particulars, role descriptions and working agreements. There are new patterns of in-service training and a growing seriousness about induction. Conscious that practice varies from place to place, we find it hard to make general statements about ordained ministry, so we descend more deeply into the particular. There are lists of competencies and skills, there is a new focus on duties and qualities, and 'Ministerial Developmental Review' identifies specific tasks and particular objectives. So, we have more and more to say about the 'task' of ministry. Pretty well every book on ministry, quite properly, pays homage to Anthony Russell's book *The Clerical Profession*, published in 1980. He identified the way a self-consciously clerical culture emerged in the nineteenth century and shows where our interest in particulars put down roots. The conversation, however, has moved on. Russell identified a professional *culture*, an attitude, emerging in the nineteenth century; now it is a professional *competence* we want, a way of doing things.[1] We were interested in what we thought about ministry, now we talk about 'outcomes', 'challenges' and 'opportunities'. In 2003 Church House Publishing published *Guidelines for the Professional Conduct of the Clergy*: 'The Church can no longer stand back from addressing the issue of what it means to act professionally in today's social climate.'[2]

The introduction of a new legal framework around the work of ordained ministry in 2011, known as 'Clergy Terms of Service', fed these assumptions and made frequent reference to 'the standards of professional conduct' (generating reams of paper about resources, appraisal and accountabilities).[3] When a new review of Continuing Ministerial Development was issued in 2009 the first page proclaimed the fact that we have entered upon a 'professional learning culture'. Latterly we have taken another step down this road in creating a Learning Community and seeking to identify an 'appropriately equipped pool of candidates with exceptional potential for the senior leadership roles in the Church's ministry'.[4]

We are more and more committed to *professionalism*, to tasks and competencies and to some managerial and executive assumptions that follow on the heels of all that. We are becoming more specific in what we expect our clergy to do. More and more diocesan and national reports first identify the context for mission and then define a solution that a renewed ministry will deliver. The task is king. The task shapes our understanding of church and ministry.

Wesley Carr

We have not always done this, but, after years of trying to define ministry by treating it as a thing set apart, we now routinely put it in context. One of the pioneers of this approach was Wesley Carr, who wrote influential books about the task and character of ministry in the 1980s.[5] Carr always had an eye to context. His own ministry began in a Luton parish and took him, eventually, to the Deanery at Westminster Abbey, but, in between, he taught ordinands at Ridley Hall and was later Diocesan Director of Training in the Chelmsford Diocese in the late 1970s and early 1980s. That was his context.

Carr's book, *The Priestlike Task*, began with context.[6] He shifted the focus away from conversations about things that are hard to measure, like holiness or providence, and concentrated instead on what the clergy do and where they do it. He did that with something of an agenda in mind. Carr thought that the Church had become self-absorbed, far too conscious of its own needs. He was determined that we should think more broadly. Specifically, he wanted us to consider the way Church and world relate to one another.[7] While the Church might like to think that it possesses something it can give to the world, the reality, Carr argued, is more complicated. He talked about the way the Church has to be 'negotiated'.[8] Here, we encounter the great theme that runs through Carr's work: he was interested in the way the Church and the world both intersect and interact. This clear focus on Church and world meant that he always understood the task in terms of the boundary between one thing and another.

The task of the Church, he argued, is to work at the boundaries of human experience, acting as an interpreter and teacher, explaining what can be said at moments when words often fail, at deathbeds and at births.[9] Following his own logic, one of his books was a study of the way the Church ministers in the occasional offices: baptism, marriage and funeral. Carr's rather formal prose masks the fact that he had been gripped by a challenge he understood to be urgent and agonizing, a need that ministry must meet at the boundaries of our expertise. The fascinating thing about Carr is that he sounds so pragmatic with his focus on task, but he keeps subverting that language. The *priestlike task*, which gives his book its title, is the agonizing business of entering into experiences where map and compass fail and summoning up resources of your own in order to offer help and a little light in the darkness

Identifying the need he saw around him, he explored the idea that ministry should set out to sustain 'dependence'. That is a difficult word to use, because some of its associations are very negative. We are rather inclined to think that *independence* equals maturity and *dependence* is cautious, insecure and, at its worst, disordered. It is what we discourage in counselling; what we denounce in those who should think for themselves. So, we need to sort out exactly what it is that Carr means. Observing that people turn to the Church when they are confronted with 'unencompassable' feelings, he suggests that there is an almost inarticulate hope that in the Church 'the uncontrollable boundary of life can be managed'.[10] Ministers have to be 'dependable'.

> There is inevitably an element of childlike dependency in the relationship to the church, and thus to its representatives, in that to some extent they are asked to solve the insoluble, cure the incurable and make reality go away.[11]

That is the context for what he had to say about 'dependence'. It is an acknowledgement that the Church will always work with a particular kind of need and that ministers have to receive this dependency. Individuals and whole communities ask the Church to do what they cannot do for themselves, to speak and act at times when words fail most people. It is in this way that Carr identified a 'task' at the heart of the life of the Church. Because this task sits at the very edges of human experience, Carr had little or nothing to say about conventional duties like preaching or the liturgy. Even his book on the occasional offices is preoccupied with debates about 'meaning', 'engagement' and 'approach'. The task is interpretation, and individual ministers will feel the weight of it. They are asked to show dependability and offer reassurance, while recognizing at times that within the Church and within themselves there is much uncertainty and confusion.

The *priestlike task* is to minister at the boundaries between church and world and to manage all the half-expressed, half-understood feelings of dependence.[12] The minister becomes what Carr called a 'consultant', someone who can interpret what others struggle to understand and can barely express. It is a tricky business. Good interpreters are gifted people; they need insight and skill. The most striking thing that Carr had to say, however, is not about the *ability* a minister needs; it is the *courage* that is required that is so striking. His use of the terms 'consultant' and 'interpreter' is slightly misleading in that it conjures up a picture of someone lifted above the heat and burden of the day. An interpreter sits to one side; a consultant often visits and departs, leaving a report behind. They are tidy people who work from the outside, looking in. What the minister does, though, is nothing like that. Carr was not interested in a ministry that hands out a diagnosis. He thought a priest is the crucible in which the whole process is worked out. The slow, hard business of interpretation does not depend on theological dictionaries, or neat and practised tricks; it has got much more to do with the energy and emotion the minister brings to any pastoral encounter. The minister uses herself, or himself, to try to understand what is happening.

A person in such a role is vulnerable. She is thrown back upon herself; upon the evidence of what she is feeling as a clue to what may be happening; upon her skill in interpreting what is happening by consistent reference to the task in hand; upon her ability to articulate what she sees and understands so that people might share that understanding; and upon her continued commitment to being all the time scrutinized by others.[13]

It is worth noting the stress Carr placed upon the minister's capacity to articulate what is happening. This task issues out into words. It is not simply a question of priests working problems out in a way that feels satisfying to them; the work has to be explained and interpreted to everyone else. Carr suggested that ministry is only effective when others can accept the interpretation that the priest provides. The priest, therefore, needs to be 'right', in the sense that she will only have authority if others accept the account the priest provides of a particular situation or a particular challenge.[14]

It is an extraordinarily demanding role that is being described here. The priest is one who never gets swept up either into the general or the particular, but always stays on the boundary. When tempted to take refuge in the simpler solutions offered by sweeping statements, or by discussing the detail, the priest must resist. Like Job's comforters, we miss the mark when we say too much or too little. We tell someone their problem is familiar because something a bit like that happened to us, or we tell them that the really interesting point is one they have missed, when they have simply asked to be understood as they are. The task of priesthood is to stay with the person and the situation, on the boundary of their experience and yours. In that uncomfortable place the priest has to learn to be prophetic. The priest has to accept dependence and yet challenge it when it is misplaced, and interpret for others the experiences that they fail to fully understand themselves.

There is a long history of books about ministry which describe attitude and approach, piety and prayer. Wesley Carr helps answer the question about what a priest should be doing. He does that by being clear that priesthood belongs to a place and time. It is an unusual, thought-provoking approach, but the definition he offers is still quite loose. Carr did not really explain what the Church is trying to achieve in all this work of interpretation. In fact, he rather set his face against there being any outcome of these encounters on the boundary. He was not (at least on the face of it) interested in mission, or redemption; he was more concerned that someone might feel understood and might be equipped to live life with a little more understanding and purpose.

The input is a series of feelings some of which are their own and some incomprehensible. The conversion is the process by which these are sorted and interpreted, so that the people concerned may better locate themselves in life with themselves, their families, their neighbours, and, we might add, with God. The output is human beings or new human units (marriages or families) which can sustain a vision of life having some meaning for themselves and others. The church and ministers serve that process. They cannot control it.[15]

He required priests to interpret, rather than teach, and committed them to what would always be work in progress.

Carr spoke at a time when we were losing our confidence in the resources we had been using for generations. Our familiar theological vocabulary had become less and less familiar to those around us. As a parish priest in a middle-class suburb in the mid-1990s, I once had to explain to a bright 9-year-old why we had a 'a man on a bit of wood', because he had never before seen a crucifix and could not summon up any image of the crucified Christ. Priests now meet people who, even in late middle age, have never encountered raw bereavement and are bewildered by it. There are conspiracies of kindness surrounding the desperately ill, who are too often discouraged from talking about what is happening to them, and asked not to cry. Carr rightly argued that the job of the priest, at moments like this, is to offer confidence and courage, honesty and whatever hope can be mustered. Priests are present and find the words. By bearing what seems unbearable they sometimes help others bear it too.

Carr was quick to notice that we repeatedly duck the challenge. One of the major problems for the Church, he noticed, is a terrible tendency to abandon the boundaries steering the middle way through middle England. Over and again the Church slides into what he calls 'private' and 'distinctively "Christian" behaviour and activity'. What he means is that churches become clubs in which Christians restrict and restrain the frame of reference, shutting the church door to keep the wolves at bay.[16] He described the way vicars can begin to think in terms of the congregation, not the parish, and the tendency for whole churches to evolve into frantic associations of mutual affirmation.[17] The stronger the experience within the charmed circle, the less interest there is in the world outside. So church and clergy can redefine the community and the risk. In *Brief Encounters*, Carr observed, rather sadly, that the clergy seem to be less eager and excited than once they were about the occasional offices, baptisms, marriages and funerals. Instead they turn to counselling and, having changed the rules, complain that no one wants to play the new game:

> One response which is sometimes heard from minsters who have acquired such training is that they seem not to meet people. Having acquired the skills of counselling they discover that people do not come for counsel ... The continuing demand for the occasional offices suggests that people may desire the church's ministry (though not necessarily counselling) while the church's minsters find it increasingly difficult to perceive that such encounters are ministry.[18]

Thirty years later we have taken the point. Our conversation about ministry is more imaginative and more courageous (though we have not rediscovered his enthusiasm for the pastoral offices). There is energy for new forms of engagement. Where once we grumbled such work was not real ministry, now we plunge into it, only pausing occasionally to wonder if it is real church. Carr's arguments are powerful and dense. He cuts to the bone in his analysis of the changing role of bishop and diocesan policy. Tackling the immense challenges of living out the mission of God, he argues that the church has not lacked ambition or enterprise; initiatives abound and strategies multiply. The danger is not a lack of effort; it lies more in the amount of time we have to spend talking to ourselves. He keeps asking hard questions about structure and practice. Suspicious of clergy who want to manage their experience, he was dubious about the pressure to become expert or professional. Yet he still wanted to remind us that the clergy do profess something. The use of the phrase 'she is going into the Church' about someone who is going to be ordained may well be unfortunate, but it does convey a truth.

> The life of a professional is chiefly characterised by the way in which the person himself and the institution he represents interact. As medicine is often discovered through an encounter with a doctor, or the law through an encounter with a lawyer or policeman, so too the minister embodies the institution he represents. He invests himself personally in his work.[19]

Carr argued, then, that the clergy are professional in the sense that they are visible and provide a route into the Church. Not entirely surprisingly, he considered that they also have a professional expertise which is exercised in the business of interpretation.

Reading Carr again transported me back to a diocesan retreat house in 1986 (and the story with which this book began). His book had only recently been published and was being much discussed. On my ordination retreat, W. H. Vanstone borrowed that language of being out on the 'boundaries' and frightened me rigid. I knew all the temptations that Carr identified and I was all for giving in to them. Ministry on the boundaries really does call, above all else, for courage. Courage becomes the defining mark of priesthood. Carr refused to accept that there could be any shelter from the storm. Everything rests on the particular moment, the situation out on whatever boundary we have reached, however terrible, where the priest and the priest's resources of faith, emotion and energy are put to the test. It is magnificent and dramatic stuff, and it has delivered, in passing, some body blows to all that is safe and self-serving.

There is a reason, though, why no other writers describe ministry in quite the same way, as a form of personal endeavour. Paring down the explicitly ecclesiastical language, Carr was clearer about the reality of each 'encounter' than about the hope and faith that we might use as interpreters (or, indeed, *ab*use and make it a kind of spiritual eiderdown to smother the moment). The analysis of context and the determination to identify a proper task is not new to Carr. We will find something similar in Gregory the Great planning serious endeavour even as he watched the city of Rome crumble around him, 'the walls going to ruin, the houses falling down, the churches destroyed by the whirlwind'.[20] What was unusual, in Carr, was his sense that our resources were personal. He was concerned that, after years of talking to ourselves, we needed to adapt and pay attention to the world around us. Gregory proposed the even more ambitious project of calling society itself to become what it is supposed to be.

Wesley Carr produced one of the most radical and exhilarating accounts of how priests engage with the world. Determined that the engagement itself should be radical and thorough, he stripped away all the resources that the clergy normally deploy. He identified a task, but few tools to do it. It is hardly surprising it gave me pause for thought on my ordination retreat and it is hardly surprising therefore that I still sometimes struggle to describe what it is I 'do'.

John Fisher

Carr gets to grips with one of the great dilemmas of ordained ministry. Setting the clergy apart, we conceive an identity for them and begin to identify the qualities we might require: holiness, empathy, resilience … The clergy then disappoint us, either because they do not match our aspirations for them or because, as we concentrate on what they should *be*, we forget to agree what it is they should *do*. Realizing our mistake and turning to what the church might actually *need*, we begin to think instead of the jobs that we might want done. We suspect that these jobs might be slightly different in, say, Runcorn in 2015 than what was needed in the thirteenth century in Rainham, or in Tudor England in the parish of St Giles Cripplegate. A different focus throws up different challenges. Clergy attentive to context and busy with tasks can then disappoint us, because they do not seem to have any sense of distinctiveness; there is no sense they might have breathed the air of a different country.

Again and again the Church has struggled with this question of the distinctiveness of role and task.

In the mid-sixteenth century this was a challenge that loomed very large indeed. In 1521, in hiding in a castle he rather grandly thought of as 'his Patmos', Luther had written a number of pamphlets developing his ideas and following the careering path of his own logic. These texts rapidly became the manifestos of reform. In one of them, *De Abroganda Missa Privata* (*Of the Abrogation of Private Masses*), he attacked private masses, the practice by which a rich, and anxious, penitent might pay to have Masses said for his or her soul after death. In particular, Luther took issue with the idea that in each and every Mass Christ's sacrifice was being offered again to God, and with the whole idea that this must be a peculiarly *priestly* practice. Determined to avoid any suggestion that we can control or administer God's grace, Luther suddenly seemed to be elbowing the work of the priesthood aside. John Fisher, Bishop of Rochester, had already identified Luther as a heretic and an enemy, and was horrified. He argued back in his own book, *Sacri Sacerdotii Defensio* (*The Defence of the Priesthood*).[21]

To make sense of what Fisher wrote, we must remember that he was in the midst of an argument that was both fundamentally important to him and also unusually brutal in character. Although Luther was a professional theologian, he entered debate more like a doberman than a don. Fisher deliberately chose not to adopt a similarly rumbustious style, but he knew he was in a fight. *The Defence of the Priesthood* is a polemical work; it is not Fisher setting out his full understanding of what priesthood is, rather he was defending the idea that we *need* priests. That is why there is such an emphasis, in what he has to say, on what is 'necessary'.

Fisher mustered his authorities: Tertullian, Augustine, Jerome, Hilary, Ambrose and more. If a choice was being offered, he was clear that he would not exchange 'the pillar and ground of truth' for the fly-by-night ideas of a radical German friar. Fisher's understanding of ministry was rooted in the historic church. In an argument we have heard before and will hear

again, he made it clear that priesthood was not a human insti-
tution that we might manipulate and mould; it had its origins in
scripture and in Christ's care for the Church. He went further,
though, urging that the priesthood was *necessary*. Necessary,
he argued, because Christians need some people set aside to
do a particular job. He piled the arguments up. Because the
faithful will always fall away from the faith, they need pastors
and guides. Because they have dull minds they need teachers.
Because they slip into sin they need monitors to keep an eye on
them. Because they are sluggish they need someone to stir them
up, and because the devil and false teachers get to work on
them they need priests to defend them. Fisher had moved deftly
from debating the authority on which ministry rests into a discussion about the authority that ministry possesses. He was a
good enough theologian to know that the case for priesthood
cannot solely rest on it being useful. Even so, it was a key element in his argument that priests were necessary because they
have a particular job to do.

Fisher had a lively way with scripture and wove Old and
New Testament texts together in stimulating, if sometimes
slightly implausible, associations. Fisher believed that the
Church was a sort of mirror to creation – a spiritual version of
the physical universe. That was an ancient and familiar idea,
explored by Clement of Alexandria and others.[22] In Fisher's
hands it allowed a lively use of biblical texts. So, Psalm 19
('The heavens are telling the glory of God') should not simply
be read as a hymn about the creator of the sun, moon and stars,
but as a hymn about the Church.

> The heavens [David] says, 'tell forth the glory of God'. For as
> the heavenly bodies in their orbits give light, heat, moisture,
> life, thunder and lightning, so do the apostles and other
> ministers carry out analogous offices. They give light by the
> example of their lives, heat by the fervour of their charity,
> moisture by their exhortations, life by the greatness of their
> promises, thunder by their warnings, lightning by their
> miracles.[23]

Fisher believed that the clergy do something distinctive and particular. He described the task in general terms: teaching, admonition, encouragement and so on. He clearly thought of the clergy as the people's champions against sin. We should notice that the consequence of all this was that Fisher always understood priesthood as belonging to the Church; the vocation of the priest is to help the Church realize its own vocation. He accepted, as scripture demanded and Luther claimed, that there is a common priesthood of all God's people, but he refused to believe that one Christian could therefore act as priest for another. Real priestly ministry, he argued, creates relationship; it is set at the service of the whole people of God and builds community.

Luther wanted to see all Christians exercising their share of the priesthood of Christ. He urged a point the Reformation developed:

> [W]hatever issues from baptism, may boast that it has been consecrated priest, bishop, and Pope, although it does not beseem everyone to exercise these offices. For, since we are all priests alike, no man may put himself forward, or take upon himself, without our consent and election, to do that which we have all alike power to do.[24]

This was a glimpse of the priesthood of all believers. The problem for Fisher was that Luther seemed so determined to ensure equality in ministry that he wanted to make everyone the same. What Fisher was defending was the idea of a Christian community that needs a diversity of gifts and in which there is always more than one task. Luther knew that the church had undersold the dignity of Christ's common people and railed at a culture that made priests not just ministers, but shareholders of grace. Fisher strove to rescue an understanding of ministry that might allow us all to take delight in difference.

Priests, professionals and paragons

In the 1980s Carr thought there was a priestlike task. In the early sixteenth century Fisher argued priesthood had distinctive functions. In the thirteenth century we trained clergy for a ministry built around confession, and in the early seventeenth century we wanted them to be preachers. We are not unfamiliar with the idea that ministry might have a special focus. The argument now takes a different form. In 2003 the Church of England published a document which is usually referred to as the Hind Report (possibly because *Formation for Ministry within a Learning Church* was not a title that made the heart beat faster). One of the assumptions that the report explored was that there was a rising expectation of ministry and the expectation was that ministry would be more and more professional: 'A further relevant factor is the continuing rising expectation of ministerial and professional competence in the clergy, an expectation coming both from the Church and from society.'[25]

In the same year, the Church also published *Guidelines for the Professional Conduct of the Clergy*. Both documents had a slightly defensive tone. The Hind Report noted that a first draft had been criticized and had been accused of capitulating 'to an understanding of priesthood that is more about educational attainment than about issues of holiness, prayer, calling, gifts in ministry, and apostolic charge'.[26] The *Guidelines* noted that 'Some believed the work to be unnecessary. God calls to ministry and the minister should need no other guidelines than the leading of the Holy Spirit.'[27]

A number of different prompts were responsible for this sudden insistence on professionalism. The Hind Report was bothered by standards of education and also looked for signs of 'competence'. It clearly had a task in mind and wanted to be sure that the clergy were equipped for that task. The *Guidelines* worried about safeguarding and wanted to be sure that the clergy understood their responsibilities to the vulnerable and weak.[28] As has already been pointed out, the trouble is that the relationship between ministry and professionalism is uneasy. Professionals have a 'practice'. They work with boundaries and constraints. The Church has learnt from them that a very serious failure to understand boundaries and constraints has inflicted terrible harm on vulnerable people who trusted the clergy and who were then failed by them. Even so, professionalism does not sum up or exhaust the expectation we have of clergy. There is an unlimited, unbrokered expectation that falls on the clergy (as on anyone who seeks to live life fully). Loving God and loving neighbour, we are all, always, going to have to be rather more than just professional.

The *Guidelines* included 'A Theological Reflection' from Francis Bridger. Ten years later it is still the last word on this tricky topic and was quoted at the beginning of the Green Report.[29] *Green* shifted the focus from professionalism to leadership, but, like the Hind Report, it still prompted critics to complain that the stress on executive ability shouldered out a once familiar hope that we would be led by theologians, pastors, prophets and evangelists.[30] This is not simply an argument about style or focus; it goes deeper than that. Carr was right, context does matter. Ministry belongs to the Church and, as the Church adapts, ministry must change. There are specific tasks that must be done in a given time and place. Here, now, the task we have identified requires us to be swift, resourceful, imaginative and decisive, and that is a task of leadership.

Tasks change, but the temptations remain the same. Always we are in danger of becoming too general, or too specific. We make ministry sound grand and dramatic and forget to spell out the task at all, or we make it too particular and lose ourselves in detail. At a time when the Church is focused on leadership those temptations are real. All the books will tell you that good leadership is both visionary and focused. It has a goal and a way of getting there. If the vision is glorious and the process is good, then we will all be blessed. Problems only come if the vision or the process is less than the gospel, less than a vision of the Kingdom of God, less than an absolute demand to love God and neighbour. Carr and Fisher wrote about task and never once surrendered the conviction that the task is always servant of a Kingdom that is yet to come. Their convictions were never constrained by a limited ambition. They understood that ministry can never be a possession, a task that we can contain, manage and complete. They subvert the idea that ministry is one thing only. For Carr it was an 'encounter', for Fisher it began and ended in the grace of God. Both of them remind us that there might be a danger that, in asking for greater professionalism or outstanding leadership, we might settle for less than we really need.

Notes

1 *Formation for Ministry within a Learning Church* (The Hind Report), London: Church House Publishing, 2003, 4.12, 4.13.

2 F. Bridger, 'A Theological Reflection', in *Guidelines for the Professional Conduct of the Clergy*, London: Church House Publishing, 2003, p. 20.

3 *Review of Clergy Terms of Service*, London: Church House Publishing, 2004, p. 8.

4 *Talent Management for Future Leaders and Leadership Development for Bishops and Deans: A New Approach*, 2014, p. 4, https://www.churchofengland.org/media/2130591/report.pdf; usually called 'The Green Report'.

5 W. Carr, *The Priestlike Task: A Model for Developing and Training the Church's Ministry*, London: SPCK, 1985; W. Carr, *Brief Encounters: Pastoral Ministry through the Occasional Offices*, London: SPCK, 1985.

6 Carr, *Priestlike Task*, pp. 3, 4.

7 Carr, *Priestlike Task*, p. 5.

8 See A. Redfern, *Ministry and Priesthood*, London: Darton, Longman & Todd, 1999, pp. 116–17.

9 Carr, *Priestlike Task*, p. 10.

10 Carr, *Priestlike Task*, p.10.

11 Carr, *Priestlike Task* (quoting W. G. Lawrence and E. J. Miller), pp. 13–14.

12 Carr, *Priestlike Task*, p. 15; *Brief Encounters*, p. 11.

13 Carr, *Priestlike Task*, pp.15, 16.

14 Carr, *Priestlike Task*, p. 23.

15 Carr, *Brief Encounters*, p. 30.

16 Carr, *Priestlike Task*, p. 25.

17 Carr, *Priestlike Task*, p. 43.

18 Carr, *Brief Encounters*, p. 3.

19 Carr, *Priestlike Task*, p. 39.

20 Gregory, *Homily in Ezekiel* 2.6.22, quoted in W. H. C. Frend, *The Rise of Christianity*, London: Darton, Longman & Todd, 1986, p. 885.

21 See R. Rex, 'The Polemical Theologian', in B. Bradshaw and E. Duffy (eds), *Humanism, Reform and Reformation: The Career of Bishop John Fisher*, Cambridge: Cambridge University Press, 1989, pp. 110–12; R. H. Bainton, *Here I Stand: A Life of Martin Luther*, Nashville TN: Abingdon Press, 1955, pp. 148–59, especially pp. 156–7.

22 Clement of Alexandria, *Paedagogus* 1.6.27, and usefully discussed in *The Catechism of the Catholic Church*, 758–60.

23 J. Fisher, *The Defence of the Priesthood*, [1525], trans. P. E. Hallett, London: Burns, Oates, Washbourne, 1935, pp. 33–4.

24 M. Luther, 'To the Christian Nobility of the German Nation', in E. G. Rupp and B. Drewery (eds), *Martin Luther: Documents of Modern History*, London: Edward Arnold, 1970, pp. 43, 44.

25 *Formation for Ministry within a Learning Church*, 4.12.

26 *Formation for Ministry within a Learning Church*, 2.3.

27 'Preface', *Guidelines for the Professional Conduct of the Clergy*, p. ix.

28 See the 'Foreword', *Guidelines for the Professional Conduct of the Clergy*.

29 *Talent Management for Future Leaders and Leadership Development*, p. 5.

30 A point made powerfully by Martyn Percy, 'Are these the leaders that we really want?', *Church Times*, 10 December 2014.

4

Outreaching Speech

Daring to hope

Late in the second century, Christians from two communities in the south of France were arrested by the Roman authorities and then tortured. Among them was a deacon, called Sanctus, from Vienne.

> While the wicked men hoped, by the continuance and severity of his tortures to wring something from him which he ought not to say, he girded himself against them with such firmness that he would not even tell his name, or the nation or city to which he belonged, or whether he was bond or free, but answered in the Roman tongue to all their questions, 'I am a Christian.'[1]

'I am a Christian,' he said; in answer to all their questions: 'I am a Christian.' Scorched, with red-hot metal plates, until he was completely disfigured, 'unlike a human form', he insisted again and again, 'I am a Christian.' It sounds like defiant commitment, but there was more to it than that, and those who wrote the account of his agony knew it. They took particular care to point out that Sanctus would say this about himself and *nothing else.* His only account of himself was, 'I am a Christian.' He offered up no name, no birthplace, no nationality and no home; it was as if he had no other identity than Christ. As the torturers set about destroying his convictions and his appearance (and with dreadful determination they returned to the task on another day), Sanctus defined himself, 'I am a Christian.'

Christian faith is always corporate, we will find our place in a kingdom, in a fellowship, a city, a wedding feast, or as part of a harvest.[2] Our true identity is shared, and Paul tells us it is rooted in Christ. Sanctus was right, his faith was more than a persuasion, it was a personality. Romans, who embraced new shrines and new cults with blithe enthusiasm, turned intolerant and aggressive when confronted by the disciples of Jesus Christ. It was the *distinctiveness* of Christian commitment that offended them. Christianity will always look *particular* to outsiders. The problem is that Christians, knowing that, so often make themselves *peculiar*. Called to make disciples of all nations, we offer an invitation to join a club. It is all done with good intention (and in the best possible taste), but churches keep acquiring a peculiar character and a style. Proclaiming the death of Christ, we make one community polite and middle class, another liberal and languid, and a third angry and impassioned, or have any number of other, particular qualities. The basic temptation in religion, the temptation to which the Pharisees succumbed, is to make faith a peculiar activity, performed by particular people. Jesus was besieged by people who wanted to know just exactly what they should do and refused to offer them the loyalty card they longed for. Eating with tax collectors and sinners, consorting with Gentiles and lepers, he challenged all those particular loyalties and activities that we relish. His family heard him summon others to be his brothers and sisters, Pharisees curled their lips as he urged principle over custom.[3]

Christians should have nothing peculiar about them. They have no special knowledge of God, they have no particular practice. Christianity is not a subset of human living, a refinement, a tweak. Christianity is life in its fullness. In Christ, we get not just a measure of what we are, we see what we should become. Christian vocation sets a future before us. It is what we *will be* that is so interesting. To use the kind of vocabulary that sets bearded theologians nodding, the church is 'eschatological', it longs for redemption. I once heard Henry Chadwick point out in a sermon that the one truly remarkable contribution that Christianity has made to the world is the doctrine of hope. For the deacon Sanctus, in his torment, hope was all that he had, but it made all the difference. He answered his torturers in the Roman tongue, speaking their language, another human being just like them, with no particular character but with the hope that the story about human being will be fulfilled in glory.[4]

When the Church and its ministry canonize careful plans to make things just slightly better they need to be sure they do not smother our hope. The good news of the gospel is not three priorities and a working group; it is repentance, forgiveness and salvation. As Herbert McCabe puts it, 'The business of the Church is to "remember" the future. Not merely to remember that there is to be a future, but mysteriously to make that future, full of grace and truth, "really present".'[5]

Irenaeus

Grace offers me an escape from all the constraints of being too particular and from being captivated by myself. This is an idea that looms large in the work of Irenaeus. Irenaeus understood that Jesus did not take flesh to be made like me; he took flesh so that I might be like *him*. It is to Irenaeus that we owe the phrase often translated as 'the glory of God is a human being fully alive': 'For the glory of God is a living man; and the life of man consists in beholding God.'[6]

Irenaeus kept insisting that what we need to know is Christ. It is therefore not really surprising (and actually rather endearing) that we know virtually nothing about Irenaeus himself. He was clearly well educated and well travelled. He tells us that he had heard Polycarp preach, and we know that Polycarp was Bishop of Smyrna in the early second century.[7] Later in life, though, Irenaeus was in Gaul, and then travelled again, carrying news to the wider Church of the terrible persecution in Lyon that swept up the deacon Sanctus and so many others. He was certainly a presbyter. He may have been made bishop in Lyon after the 90-year-old Pothinus died as a result of a beating in the persecution.

Irenaeus was a witness to persecution. He wrote for a church under attack from without. Interestingly, what frightened him more was the threat of error from within. His great work was an assault on false teaching: *Adversus Omnes Haereses,* (Against Heresies).[8] The book ranged widely, but there was also a focused concern, because Irenaeus nurtured a particular, passionate loathing for Gnosticism. Gnosticism is a tricky thing to try to describe. It is older than Christian faith and it takes many forms. At its simplest, however, it is that subtle, beguiling desire to turn faith into a possession. What Gnosticism teaches is that really religious people know things that no one else could possibly know. It is the possession of knowledge that marks the Gnostics out (in Greek, knowledge is *gnōsis*). It is knowledge that distinguishes Gnostics from Christians.

Christians, of course, *do* know something. They know Christ. There are no secrets in Christ; he taught publicly, died publicly and showed himself at the resurrection. He revealed things. Christians are people who know what was revealed in Christ and know that they know nothing more. Christians know that they do not 'know' God. The Gnostics begged to differ. They knew secrets; they had peered into the deep mysteries of the origin of the universe and the mind of God. Their ideas and stories sound ludicrous and strange now. Their faith was a cocktail of myth and mystery. What made the Gnostics dangerous, however, was that they used those ideas to explain away problems that other Christians found difficult. They 'knew' where evil came from; they could describe the human soul. The explanations may have been no better than a fairy tale, but it was a beguiling fairy tale, recounted with conviction. Many of us are fairly easily conned by people who confidently declare that they know how things work. The woman who can tell me which sequence of dialogue boxes to open on my computer and the man who approaches my car with some fancy spanner get my respect. I am so relieved to encounter some confidence that I do not always stop to ask the important questions about their credentials and *how* they came by this information.

Irenaeus, well aware of just how dangerous all this was, and acute in his observation, asked the hard questions about how any of us know what is true and how we know what to trust. He held that two truths were paramount. First, the Church speaks with one voice, everywhere. There could be no secret teaching, no separate tradition. Second, the truth that the Church proclaims is certain and sure and the tradition of the Church is the guarantee.

> The Church, having received this preaching and this faith, although scattered throughout the whole world, yet, as if occupying but one house, carefully preserves it. She also believes these points [of doctrine] just as if she had but one soul, and one and the same heart, and she proclaims them, and teaches them, and hands them down, with perfect harmony, as if she possessed only one mouth.[9]

Irenaeus had a lot to say about a tradition that is 'steadfast', 'one and the same way of salvation is shown throughout the whole world'.[10] There are, in short, no 'versions' of the truth. He argued that, in sustaining the one truth everywhere, the ministry of the Church had a crucial role. It had to teach the one faith and hand it on, safely, one to the other. The continuity of the ministry, the physical continuity of one bishop succeeding to the chair of another, and the intellectual continuity of one bishop teaching the same faith that his predecessor taught, is the mark and guarantee of the true Church.[11] As a consequence, Irenaeus made lists, demonstrating a known succession in Rome: 'Linus ... To him succeeded Anacletus; and after him, in the third place from the apostles, Clement ... To this Clement there succeeded Evaristus. Alexander followed Evaristus; then, sixth from the apostles, Sixtus was appointed ...'[12]

This kind of list gives the clergy a decisive role. Irenaeus mentioned people by name. He knew that faith prompts real people to work out their salvation in particular places. All of us share the calling to live life fully in Christ. What the clergy do is to help make the tradition visible; they summon us into unity by giving unity a character here and now. They do not determine what the teaching is (that is the Gnostic way of those who have insights of their own). The clergy receive truth, articulate it for the here and now, and pass it on. The tradition is not written in ink and paper and rewritten, it is etched in the heart.[13]

The principle is simple: the Church is a glimpse of the Kingdom into which we are summoned, a hint of the great and
glorious future in community. The principle is simple; it is the
practice that is the challenge. The Church may be a glimpse of
the Kingdom, but the reality is often a bit disappointing. The
problem we have is the problem that Irenaeus identified. It is a
problem with the way a general invitation becomes particular,
and it is very often a problem that dogs the clergy. Try as we
might, we are limited. What Irenaeus argued so passionately
was that the Church proclaims the whole truth, and proclaims
it everywhere. That task, though, falls to particular people,
who have particular skills and particular experiences. Even the
best of the clergy can only communicate a little of the glory of
God and always make it specific in ways that appeal to some
people and not others.

We are all of us gloriously peculiar. The clergy, and others,
cannot help but proclaim the summons to the Kingdom in the
accents of Weybridge or of Wakefield. There is nothing wrong
in that, so long as we are all aware that it is not the peculiarity
that is important. We need our clergy to be individuals with
names like David, or Dawn, doing the best they can to model
their own lives on Christ. They must never think of themselves
as celebrities, as though their character and experience might
be normative for others. Trying to be too priestly the clergy
can forget to be human, but then, attempting to be engaging,
they can be too personal and peculiar. Ministry must always
summon us into the generous truths that are everywhere
and for all. Ministry must strive to set the hope of the whole
Kingdom before us.

Ignatius

This preoccupation with identity surfaces in the work of St
Ignatius of Antioch and prompts an extraordinary series of
letters that have had a profound effect on our ideas about
ministry. Ignatius was the second, or perhaps the third, Bishop
of Antioch and there, close to the end of the first century, he

was sentenced to death (probably between 98 and 117).[14] He was sent to Rome, under armed guard, so that he could be thrown to the animals in the arena. As he made the journey towards his death, he wrote letters to a number of churches close to the Aegean and to Rome.

The letters are important documents. They are also a little controversial. Modern readers of the letters are often puzzled by Ignatius' attitude to death. He embraced the idea of his own martyrdom with what can look like slightly wild-eyed enthusiasm. In the letter to the Romans, Ignatius famously begged that no effort should be made to save him:

> I shall willingly die for God, unless ye hinder me ... I am the wheat of God, and let me be ground by the teeth of the wild beasts, that I may be found the pure bread of Christ. Rather entice the wild beasts, that they may become my tomb.[15]

The letters also have quite a lot to say about bishops, and Ignatius (who was himself a bishop) can sound peremptory and even pompously insistent on a bishop's dignity: 'To those who indeed talk of the bishop, but do all things without him ... such persons seem to me not possessed of a good conscience, but to be simply dissemblers and hypocrites.'[16] He urged the churches into obedience to the bishop: 'Be ye subject to the bishop as to the Lord, for "he watches for your souls, as one that shall give account to God".'[17] Christian communities were to show the bishop 'reverence' and 'do nothing without him'.[18] Ignatius knew that faith and unity were at risk and knew that someone had to urge both. So the claims he made for the bishop are grandiose: 'I exhort you to study to do all things with a divine harmony, while your bishop presides in the place of God.'[19] In an age when bishops have grown wary of the temptations of office, and look alarmed when someone calls them 'My Lord', Ignatius sounds downright odd.

The truth is that he was passionate about his ministry; he knew it made a difference. We must not miss the point Ignatius was making. His letters were clear that, while ministry mattered, some things mattered more. Indeed, one thing mattered above all else. Ignatius wanted the Church to talk about Jesus Christ. He rehearsed the story that has to be told:

> He was the Son of God, 'the first-born of every creature,' God the Word, the only-begotten Son, and was of the seed of David according to the flesh, by the Virgin Mary; was baptized by John, that all righteousness might be fulfilled by Him; that He lived a life of holiness without sin, and was truly, under Pontius Pilate and Herod the tetrarch, nailed [to the cross] for us in His flesh.[20]

It was not just that this is a great confession of faith, the sort of thing that bishops ought to say. Ignatius was convinced that Christ is our blueprint. From Christ, as Ignatius put it, 'we derive our being'. Apart from Christ we will never have 'true life'.

Ignatius wrote about what life in Christ looked like, and he wrote about unity.[21] So far, so good, but there was a difficulty. While Ignatius knew what to look for, he struggled to find the right words to describe it. Like Irenaeus, 80 years after him, he found the faith was being contested. Challenges came from people who used very similar language to orthodox Christians; the wells had been poisoned. That is why he insisted on the role of the bishop, and on the unity of the presbyters and deacons who worked with him. He was not making a point about the status of bishops, he was insisting on the unity they can guarantee, a common unity in Christ.

> I exhort you to study to do all things with a divine harmony, while your bishop presides in the place of God, and your presbyters in the place of the assembly of the apostles, along with your deacons, who are most dear to me, and are entrusted with the ministry of Jesus Christ, who was with the Father before the beginning of time.[22]

Of course, that makes the work of a bishop a huge responsibility, and commentators have noticed something slightly odd about Ignatius. For all his apparent confidence in what bishops might do, he seemed to think that they might do it best when they are quietest. So, in the passionately enthusiastic letter to the Ephesians we find Ignatius saying, 'The more, therefore, you see the bishop silent, the more do you reverence him.'[23] That letter to the Ephesians knows the value of silence; 'It is better for a man to be silent and be [a Christian], than to talk and not to be one.'[24] The point here is that, for all the importance of words, it is not what we *say* that matters. The offering we make to God is our lives, and a silent holiness is more welcome than a rackety and talkative confusion. There is, though, another reason for silence. Ignatius knew that words keep saying too much or too little:

> Now the virginity of Mary was hidden from the prince of this world, as was also her offspring, and the death of the Lord; three mysteries of renown, which were wrought in silence, but have been revealed to us.[25]

'Wrought in silence', Ignatius knows that there is a height and depth, a distance and a mystery we cannot describe.

Ignatius was a theologian wrestling not just with questions of church order and hierarchy, but also with religious language. He knew that language could fall short of its aim and, worse still, he knew language can deceive. The fundamental problem, he suggested, is that we keep talking about the wrong thing:

> [T]he spirit of deceit preaches himself, and speaks his own things, for he seeks to please himself. He glorifies himself, for he is full of arrogance. He is lying, fraudulent, soothing, flattering, treacherous, rhapsodical, trifling, inharmonious, verbose, sordid, and timorous.[26]

Christians are the people who have been given the words of life. It is curious, then, that so many Christians want to talk not about Christ but about themselves. Our conversation has become strangely self-absorbed; we talk about ourselves too much. My experience is, in truth, radically different from yours, and the way of salvation is not for you to become more like me (that really would not be good for you). The gospel is about Jesus Christ. We will grow into a mature faith and into unity when we all long to be one in Christ. He, and he alone, has shown us what it means to be truly human. Copying one another, talking about ourselves, we miss the point entirely. Clergy need to learn this restraint.

I tried this idea out on a colleague while this book was still a draft. My text came back to me covered in increasingly passionate scribbling. I had touched a nerve, and I had failed to make a distinction that is significant. Christian faith is rooted in real life, in particular places and at certain times. We return again and again to tell the story of a baby born in Bethlehem and of a man dying in agony on a cross on Golgotha. The heart of Christian conviction is the extraordinary claim that the life of God is seen and understood in our human life. We do not meet God in a book, or by being good, or by having visions in the night. We know God because he has shown himself to us in the one way we might really understand. God has lived as one of us. Now we are called to live that same life ourselves. We should constantly apply the gospel to life. Not only can we make connections between the glory of God and our daily lives, we *must* do that. In truth, it is God, not the devil, who is in the detail. So, our feelings and our experiences are indeed part of the raw materials of faith. We *can* talk about ourselves and we must. What we have to guard against, however, is the dreadful tendency to make our own experience and our own lives the benchmark for what is best and what is true. At the point of crisis in his ministry, in Gethsemane, Christ was tempted to do just that. He was tempted to take control of the situation, tempted to impose himself and tempted to make his own will and wishes his map and compass. He resisted that temptation: 'yet, not my will, but yours be done' (Luke 22.42). Christ gave glory to God and salvation to us by resolutely refusing to make the most of himself. He gave himself up to his captors, gave his spirit up to God upon the cross. He showed us that being fully human is not the same thing as clinging on to life.

So we speak of being human, but of being human as Christ was human. It is Christ's humanity, not mine, that is definitive. This is one of the reasons why liturgy is so important. In the tested words of worship we stop speaking about ourselves. We tune our voices together, learn to speak a common tongue and anticipate the worship of heaven when we will at last speak in harmony. We can have confidence in these words. At funerals and at weddings, at altars and at fonts, there are words we can use. And these are words we need. Tongue-tied and inarticulate, both when we are grief-stricken and when we are joyful, we need the words that are given to us. There is a good poem by Anne Stevenson, called 'The Minister', which recognizes the real significance of having someone to speak the words. The poem asks what need there is for a minister at a funeral. After all, the minister will not dig the hole, or wipe his eyes; bake cakes, or take care of the children. You need a minister to ensure

the words will know where to go.[27]

They need to be the right words, strong enough to bear the weight of meaning put upon them. We must not drag holy things through the dust. At a funeral years ago I heard a preacher describe life as being like an onion. We have to pass, he said, through layer after layer. 'And so', he concluded, describing a dear friend's death, 'she has broken through the last ring of the onion and emerged glorious on the draining board of the kitchen of the kingdom of heaven.' As a metaphor it did not work then and it hasn't improved with age. We must not sell the Kingdom short. I was savaged, quite properly and very memorably, by Richard Holloway when I was a student at theological college and had written a first draft of a sermon that drew on A. A. Milne with a whimsical reference to a famous teddy bear. 'I looked for the wildness of grace, and what did I get?' Richard Holloway said and fixed me with a baleful glare, 'Winnie-the-bloody-Pooh'. I don't think I have ever have mentioned Pooh, or Piglet, in a sermon since. The gospel of our redemption is a story for all ages, but it is not children's fiction. Nor is it 'a bit like' *Eastenders*.

The seventeenth-century theologian Benjamin Whichcote once suggested, 'if it were not for sin, we should converse together as angels do'.[28] The words come out wrong. As a priest, I have said too little and been too diffident. I am ashamed of that, but I am the more appalled at the memory of all those moments when I said too much and used words that were careless. Oddly, it can be my very desire to be 'priestly' that can trip me up. Eager to prove that I have a contribution to make, determined to appear theologically informed and wise, I can rush in with judgements that are wide of the mark. Even George Herbert, a man for whom words would dance, used to begin his sermons acknowledging the impossibility of the task. 'How shall we dare to appear before thy face, who are contrary to thee in all we call thee?'[29] R. S. Thomas had it right when he suggested that when we break out of silence 'something is lost'.[30]

Cyprian to be found with Christ

We live in a world of choice. I have the luxury, denied to millions, of choosing how to spend some of my time and some of my money. I am bombarded with choices and I have adjusted and adapted so that I can survive in the carnival of possibilities. I am glad of that; I can pick up the television remote control without suffering an existential crisis. The trouble is that in adjusting to the process of making so many choices something has happened to my sense of occasion. What I often forget is that choices are momentous encounters with temptation. The real danger of heresy lies in the fact that it offers a choice (which is what the Greek word *heresy* means). Jeremy Taylor pointed out that heresy is not a problem in our understanding 'but an error of the will'.[31] So, when theologians write against heresy it is the business of dangerous and deceitful choices that worries them.

Caution is more easy where danger is manifest, and the mind is prepared beforehand for the contest when the adversary avows himself. The enemy is more to be feared and to be guarded against, when he creeps on us secretly; when, deceiving by the appearance of peace, he steals forward by hidden approaches.[32]

When the Church is divided and itself offers choices, we are all at risk.

In 250 Fabian, Bishop of Rome, was a victim in the Decian persecution. Eight years later, one of his successors, Sixtus II, was arrested while presiding over worship in the catacombs and subsequently beheaded. Rome remained a focus for the Christian Church, but, in this turmoil, it was a North African bishop, Cyprian of Carthage, who emerged as a senior and authoritative spokesman for the faith. Persecution had by now divided the Church into two communities: those who had, and those who had not, compromised with the Roman authorities. Each community administered its own sacraments, so believers were baptized into one or the other, and all of them argued about whether or not there was anything authentically Christian about their opponents. Cyprian faced schism. With so much at stake, his language pulled no punches:

> Whoever is separated from the Church and is joined to an adulteress, is separated from the promises of the Church; nor can he who forsakes the Church of Christ attain to the rewards of Christ. He is a stranger; he is profane; he is an enemy. He can no longer have God for his Father, who has not the Church for his mother.[33]

There was no grace to be had; there were no true sacraments outside the one Church. The gates of salvation might be open wide, but it was still a narrow way to get there. It became an urgent matter to know whether or not you belonged to this unique community of faith. The test that Cyprian, Bishop of Carthage, applied was, unsurprisingly, episcopal. The source and foundation of unity was the bishop.

In Cyprian's hands the debate about ministry moved on in two significant ways. First, he had a particular approach, shaped by the language of the Old Testament and the Epistle to the Hebrews. The language of priesthood was already familiar

48

of course, but it had been commonplace to identify the whole Christian community as being priestly. That, after all, was what the First Epistle of Peter had suggested: 'let yourselves be built into a spiritual house, to be a holy priesthood, to offer spiritual sacrifices acceptable to God through Jesus Christ'.[34] Justin had argued that all Christians should regard themselves as 'the true high priestly race of God', and Tertullian insisted on the point.[35] Cyprian, however, laid stress on the *distinctive* priesthood of Christ:

> For who is more a priest of the most high God than our Lord Jesus Christ, who offered a sacrifice to God the Father, and offered that very same thing which Melchizedek had offered, that is, bread and wine, to wit, His body and blood?[36]

Christ's sacrifice is the controlling idea here. It is *particularly* the work of Christ to offer sacrifice. To make any sense of Cyprian, this is the crucial point. Writing about Cyprian, talking about Cyprian, the emphasis keeps falling on what he has to say about priests and bishops. For Cyprian himself the emphasis fell on Christ. Christ carries us; we put him on as we might put on a garment.[37] Our vocation is to follow his example: 'To put on the name of Christ, and not to go in the way of Christ, what else is it but a mockery of the divine name, but a desertion of the way of salvation.'[38]

Cyprian believed that bishops and presbyters share directly in the priesthood of Christ. So (and this was a very significant step to take), a bishop, or a presbyter, is a priest (*sacerdos*) in a way that other members of the church are not.

> For if Jesus Christ, our Lord and God, is Himself the chief priest of God the Father, and has first offered Himself a sacrifice to the Father, and has commanded this to be done in commemoration of Himself, certainly that priest truly discharges the office of Christ, who imitates that which Christ did; and he then offers a true and full sacrifice in the Church to God the Father, when he proceeds to offer it according to what he sees Christ Himself to have offered.[39]

Cyprian claimed that bishops and presbyters offer the sacrifice of Christ. There was more. He went on to argue that, just as the bishop imitates Christ's priesthood – and sets that priesthood before us again – so the bishop also represents the unity of the Church. Ignatius had said something not so very different, but Cyprian was urging the point in a more striking way. It is not just that we need to be obedient to bishops for the sake of unity; we need to see that bishops *are* that unity. Indeed, bishops represent unity so vividly that they truly *are* the Church. Just like Peter, who acknowledged that separation from Christ is unthinkable, 'Lord, to whom can we go?' (John 6.68), we cannot separate from the Church in the person of the bishop.

> [Y]ou ought to know that the bishop is in the Church, and the Church in the bishop; and if any one be not with the bishop, that he is not in the Church ... the Church, which is Catholic and one, is not cut nor divided, but is indeed connected and bound together by the cement of priests who cohere with one another.[40]

We are dealing with typology here. In Matthew's Gospel, when Jesus spoke of his coming death he spoke of Jonah: 'For just as Jonah was for three days and three nights in the belly of the sea monster, so for three days and three nights the Son of Man will be in the heart of the earth.'[41] In this theology, the story of Jonah becomes a 'type' of the story of Christ. Something of the importance and significance of Christ is revealed to us in the story of Jonah. Types became very important in the church. The idea that one event, or one person, belonging to a particular time could represent a truth from another time took root. In Cyprian's theology Melchizedek was a type of Christ and, even more significantly, the bishop became a type of the Church. A bishop was not just important because he did important work, but also because he represented the Church. In a sense, he *was* the Church. It was an argument that is still debated. Cyprian was a controversial character, his epistles bristle with argument. In his theology of episcopacy and in the link he forged between the sacrificial work of Christ and the eucharistic sacrifice offered by the clergy he is widely credited with creating (or ruining) our understanding of ministry. Thanks to Cyprian the clergy could claim that they alone can do what Christ himself did. Cyprian made ministry turn on the Eucharist and depend on the clergy. He put the clerical cart before the horse.

That said, Cyprian never abandoned his fundamental conviction that our vocation is not to tell Christ's story, but live it. We must be human as he was human. Of course, even in Christ's passionate and eventful life there were experiences that he never knew. He was not a woman, and never an old man. Christ did not live life *exhaustively*. We all of us do and feel things he did not know and did not feel, but he did live this life *definitively*. Christ's great command to us is the command that first called the apostles: 'Follow me.' Our great desire, as Cyprian put it, must be 'to wish to be found with Christ, to imitate that which Christ both taught and did'.[42] Here is a vocation not just for the clergy, but for us all. We are to find our life in Christ. Quoting St Paul, 'As many of you as were baptized into Christ have clothed yourselves with Christ', Cyprian insisted that all of us are summoned into the likeness of Christ.[43] We hear him assert the importance of ministry; we must also hear him remind us that the dignity is borrowed.

John Keble – why do we have priests?

The clergy point beyond themselves, away from themselves. That insight shaped the work of Irenaeus, Ignatius and Cyprian and surfaces again and again in the theology of ministry. It is found too in the work of John Keble. Famous now for his Assize Sermon and his association with the Oxford Movement, Keble was most famous in his own day for the poems he published in *The Christian Year*. For all his fame, he thought of himself as a parish priest. In tiny Gloucestershire villages, and then in Hursley, near Winchester, where he worked for 30 years, Keble dedicated most of his life to parochial ministry. It was from the pulpit at Hursley, on the Third Sunday in Advent, that he looked out across the congregation and said:

I am going to ask you a question, which concerns you and me as nearly as possible. It is just this. Why am I standing here at this moment? ... In one word, what is the use of the clergy?[44]

They must have craned forward a little in their seats as Keble posed this question. Here was Keble laying bare his own vocation.

The fact that it was the Third Sunday in Advent is significant. The collect for the Third Sunday in Advent, is a prayer about ministry:

O Lord Jesus Christ, who at thy first coming didst send thy messenger to prepare thy way before thee; Grant that the ministers and stewards of thy mysteries may likewise so prepare and make ready thy way ...

Prompted by his Prayer Book, Keble thought about the ministry and asked, 'What is a priest for?'

What is the use of the clergy? To be kind and helpful in such ways as they can, to wait on people in the way of bodily charity, to persuade people to be quiet and orderly, decent and moral?[45]

He piled up the possibilities: teaching was one thing the clergy could do; preaching peace was another. But,

There is another thing to be thought of, without which all will go wrong: and that is the end of our ministry, the prize and purpose of our calling. If we do not bear that in mind ... Christ will not be glorified, nor his people profited. Well, what is the end of our ministry? What but the salvation of souls.[46]

This was the heart of the matter. Again and again Keble preached on ministry, and again and again he made this point. He had one fundamental concern and that was with our salvation.

Keble was a scholar. He produced editions of the works of Richard Hooker and Thomas Wilson; he wrote a book on eucharistic adoration; he helped edit *The Library of the Fathers* and translated the five books of St Irenaeus' *Against Heresy*. He was also a faithful pastor. One account of his life talks of the 'gritty realism' of his parochial work.[47] Yet, when he gave an account of what ministry was, he set the claims of both learning and pastoral work in a broader, grander context. What really interested Keble was presenting his parishioners perfect in Jesus Christ:

> This and nothing short of this is the use, the purpose, the end of the clergy. As the Father sent [Christ] so he sent His Apostles, and through them His servants, the Bishops and pastors of His Church, to work under Him, for the same end, for which He came into the world, that the world through Him might be saved ... Our teaching, our preaching, our prayers, our Sacraments, our visits from house to house, whatever we do as clergymen has no meaning unless there be a day of Judgement. It is all in order to that one day.[48]

Preaching in Advent, when the church has always thought about 'Last Things', Keble spoke of judgement and salvation. The clergy, he argued, are 'Heralds warning of his coming'. Church spires were 'a silent finger pointing towards Him Who is there, watching all your ways'. In a particularly powerful passage within this sermon on the ministry, he imagined the clergy of England presenting their congregations to Christ. He imagined a day 'when the under shepherds shall all stand before Him, the chief Shepherd to give an account of you the sheep, one by one'.[49] The task of ministry was to set before a parish the reality of judgement and the hope of salvation.

The question Keble asks, 'Why do we have priests?', is not asked all that often. We ask ordinands, 'What makes you think you have a vocation to priesthood?' We ask ourselves, and one another, 'What is your strategy? What are you going to do?' As a consequence, when we discuss ministry we either use personal vocabulary – 'my' vocation, 'my' ministry – or we make lists (that tend to get longer and longer) of the things that the clergy do. Keble challenges both conversations by offering the conviction that there might be an absolute priority that informs everything else. That priority is salvation.

Christ's challenge was simple: 'Follow me.' He did not add anything about bringing the vicar along. One answer to that strange and glaring omission in God's mission strategy is to argue that Christ did say something about ministry when he appointed apostles. There are any number of theologians who make that point. More fruitful, though, has been the work of those who have noticed that in setting out to follow Christ we head in different directions. Christ summons us into the Kingdom, and a kingdom is a place where people live together. Our unity matters. Clergy must remind us of our shared vocation. The Kingdom is a destination; we need it setting before us. As Irenaeus suggested, we need people who will put our hope into words. Keble understood both points. He knew about our unity in Christ:

> becoming one of us, Bone of our bone, and Flesh of our flesh, Himself took all our infirmities: His single appearing for us before God is as if we all appeared; we are all gathered or summed up in Him.[50]

He also knew that we needed to be reminded, again, and again about the scope and scale of our hope.

Pointing at salvation is not the same thing as being expert in salvation. Keble was at pains to make it clear that he only had confidence in the clergy because he trusted in Christ. At the altar, priests know where authority lies: 'It is He Who gives it by their hands, as by their hands He made it what it is, by their hands He offers it to His Father. It is His doing not at all theirs.'[51] However important it is to have priests, whatever dignity Keble saw in the office of priest, he knew it always pointed away from itself. Indeed, Keble reminded us that we all share in a common priesthood: 'We are all priests then'; all of us have a common vocation to holiness, all of us are called to a common sacrifice.[52] The salvation that awaits is one in which all of us, priests and people, have a place. Keble believed in the drama of salvation and knew that it sweeps up us all. Recognizing that priests preach redemption as much to themselves as to others, he avoided the pitfalls of clericalism and described a common vocation.

There is a memorial to Keble in Fairford, not far from the home he once occupied, in Court Close. It contains lines he wrote for John the Baptist in *The Christian Year* and sums up his conviction that the vocation of a priest was significant, but never an end in itself:

So glorious let Thy Pastors shine,
That by their speaking lives the world may learn.[53]

Priests do not exist to make the Church slightly better; they exist to remind the Church of its goal and purpose. They do it, as Keble urges, because salvation matters.

Speech and silence

This hope for the future is a hope that the clergy have to put into words. That is the great challenge – to find the right words. Again and again Jesus began his parables with a familiar formula: 'The kingdom of heaven is like treasure hidden in a field'; 'The kingdom of heaven is like a landowner who went out early in the morning' (Matthew 13.44; 20.1). His preaching gave hope a shape and an identity. When John the Divine caught a glimpse of an open heaven he did not just see something, he heard it. 'I heard a voice from heaven like the sound of many waters and like the sound of loud thunder.'[54] When the Holy Spirit fell upon the apostles at Pentecost the crowds in Jerusalem were startled, not by what they saw but by what they heard. 'At this sound the crowd gathered and was bewildered, because each one heard them speaking in the native language of each.'[55] The Spirit, which equips and excites every ministry in the church, speaks. The Christian vocation demands that we find the right words

Speech and silence – we need to know that we can say too little or too much. On 9 July 1917, *HMS Vanguard* was moored on the north shore of Scapa Flow. Miles from the guns of the Western Front, a summer night gathered slowly and quietly over the Orkneys. Then, a terrible explosion shattered the night. Quickly searchlights swept the waves, but *HMS Vanguard* had gone. It is likely that deteriorating cordite on board *Vanguard* was responsible for the catastrophe. She was one of the largest ships in the fleet and that night there were, they say, 845 men aboard. Just two survived. The following day there was terrible work to be done. Young midshipmen were sent out on to the shore with buckets, to clear the beaches of body parts. After the war, the same young men were offered the chance of a college education in Cambridge, and Rudyard Kipling wondered what they would make of life in quiet courts by the river Cam:

> They have touched a knowledge outreaching speech
>   – as when the cutters were sent
> To harvest the dreadful mile of beach after the Vanguard
>   went.[56]

'They have touched a knowledge outreaching speech.' Christians have a language to use and they have a vocation to speak, but they should also keep falling silent. Like Isaiah in the Temple, like Moses at the burning bush, like Ezekiel, like Daniel, like St Paul, we need to know that we can stumble over our lines and mangle the words that have their beginning in the Word. We speak of things greater than we know. Words badly chosen, words spoken too soon or too late, and too many or too few, can betray the truth. There is speech, but sometimes there really needs to be silence.

The truth is that we will take any opportunity we can to make a story out of something and to put ourselves firmly in the middle of that story. We impose ourselves. Our conversation about ministry is increasingly now a conversation about ourselves, and about our personalities and our gifts. A ministry seen in terms of competencies and outcomes, a ministry explored on the basis of selection criteria, a ministry that identifies key skills and nurtures them in a Learning Community, is deeply serious about the task but might be in danger of mistaking the experience for the hope. I have heard people talk about 'my ministry' as if ministry might be something I determine, forgetting it is a call from Christ to live life in his body, the Church. Irenaeus, Ignatius and John Keble all remind us that we must not talk too much about ourselves. There really is only one life worth living, and it is the life of Christ. He is the Word, he is what we talk about. At the heart of Christian vocation is an absolute determination to point away from ourselves.

Notes

1 Eusebius, *Church History*, V. 1.20, trans. A. C. McGiffert, *N&PNF* 2S, 1.

2 Matthew 13.31; 1 John 1.3; Revelation 21.2; Revelation 19.9; 1 Corinthians 3.9.

3 See Tom Wright, *Jesus and the Victory of God*, London: SPCK, 1996, pp. 428–38.

4 John 17.22.

5 H. McCabe, *Law, Love and Language*, London: Sheed & Ward, 1968, p. 141.

6 Irenaeus, *Against Heresies*, IV.20.7, *ANF*, 1.

7 D. Minns, *Irenaeus: An Introduction*, London: Geoffrey Chapman, 1994, pp. 1–12.

8 Originally written in Greek, it survived only in a Latin translation. It is also known by the longer title, *A Refutation and Subversion of Knowledge falsely so called*.

9 Irenaeus, *Against Heresies*, I.10.2.

10 Irenaeus, *Against Heresies*, V.20.1.

11 Irenaeus, *Against Heresies*, IV.26.2.

12 Irenaeus, *Against Heresies*, III.3.3.

13 Irenaeus, *Against Heresies*, III.4.2.

14 S. Tugwell OP, *Apostolic Fathers*, London: Geoffrey Chapman, 1989, p. 105.

15 Ignatius, *Romans*, 4, *ANF*, 1.

16 Ignatius, *Magnesians*, 4, *ANF*, 1.

17 Ignatius, *Trallians*, 2, *ANF*, 1. He is quoting Hebrews 13.17.

18 Ignatius, *Magnesians*, 3; *Smyrneans*, 8, *ANF*, 1.

19 Ignatius, *Magnesians*, 6.

20 Ignatius, *Smyrneans*, 1, and see *Trallians*, 10.

21 Ignatius, *Trallians*, 4, *ANF*, 1.

22 Ignatius, *Magnesians*, 6.

23 Ignatius, *Ephesians*, 6, *ANF*, 1.

24 Ignatius, *Ephesians*, 15.

25 Ignatius, *Ephesians*, 19.

26 Ignatius, *Ephesians*, 9.

27 A. Stevenson, 'The Minister', *The Collected Poems 1955–1995*, Oxford: Oxford University Press, 1996, p. 62.

28 B. Whichcote, *Moral and Religious Aphorisms*, 1753, London: Elkin Matthews & Marrot, 1930, no. 731.

29 G. Herbert, 'The Author's Prayer Before Sermon', in F. E. Hutchinson (ed.), *The Works of George Herbert*, Oxford: Clarendon Press, 1953, p. 288.

30 R. S. Thomas, 'Kneeling', *Collected Poems 1945–1990*, London: J. M. Dent, 1993, p. 199.

31 J. Taylor, *The Liberty of Prophesying*, 2.8, in Jeremy Taylor, *The Whole Works*, ed. R. Heber, revised C. P. Eden (London 1862), p. 382.

32 Cyprian, *On the Unity of the Church*, 1, trans. E. Wallis, ANF, 5, 'Treatises of Cyprian', X.

33 Cyprian, *On the Unity of the Church*, 6.

34 1 Peter 2.5.

35 Justin Martyr, *Dialogue with Trypho*, 116; Tertullian, *De Monogamia*, 8.7.

36 Cyprian, *Epistle*, 62.4, ANF, 5.

37 J. D. Lawrence, *'Priest' as Type of Christ*, New York: Peter Lang, 1984, pp. 111, 160–1.

38 Cyprian, *Treatise X: On Jealousy and Envy*, 12, ANF, 5.

39 Cyprian, *Epistle*, 62.14.

40 Cyprian *Epistle*, 68.8

41 Matthew 12.40.

42 Cyprian, *Epistle*, 55.1.

43 Cyprian, *Epistle*, 59.2.

44 J. Keble, *Sermons for the Christian Year: Advent to Christmas*, Oxford: 1884, p. 352.

45 Keble, *Sermons*, p. 352.

46 Keble, *Sermons*, p. 353.

47 *Dictionary of National Biography* (available online).

48 Keble, *Sermons*, pp. 354–5.

49 Keble, *Sermons*, p. 361.

50 Keble, *Sermons*, p. 335.

51 Keble, *Sermons*, p. 338.

52 Keble, *Sermons*, p. 340.

53 J. Keble, 'St John Baptist's Day', in *The Christian Year*, 4th edn, 1828, p. 307.

54 Revelation 14.2.

55 Acts 2.6.

56 From R. Kipling, *The Scholars*, Garden City NY: Doubleday, Page & Co., 1927. I am indebted to Dr Jeffrey Lewin who helped me track down the reference.

5

Putting Priests in Their Place

Authority and consent

In A. N. Wilson's novel *Unguarded Hours* Norman Shotover, in training for ordained ministry, is sent on a placement to a Surrey parish. He arrives at the Vicarage (not far from the Freezer Food Centre), to meet Mr Dumble, the incumbent.

> The Dumbles were quiet people with false teeth on the National Health and an uncomplicated belief in the Four Last Things. Their favourite television programme was *Dr Finlay's Caseboook* and, although they voted Labour at the last general election, they thought it was a pity that Sir Alec could not be Prime Minister.
> 'Daddy's in the greenhouse,' said Mrs Dumble, when Norman appeared at the door. 'The chrysanthemums have been a real joy to him this year.'[1]

Mr Dumble is a particular kind of priest, in a fawn cardigan, knitted by his wife. He belongs to a time and a place. The joke, the terrible joke, is that he is supposed to be so much more than that. We require Mr Dumble to come out of his greenhouse and point the way to the Kingdom of God. We doubt that he can do it.

Context matters, but context must not be master; ministry must live *in* a community without being entirely *of* the community. Herbert McCabe thought that ordination requires a priest to spend a lifetime asking how *this* can turn into *that*; to be 'A revolutionary whose job is the subversion of the world through the preaching of the gospel ... He is the leader of his people in a movement to a new community.'[2]

The pages of literature are stuffed with clergy who fail. The fawning Mr Collins in *Pride and Prejudice*, Anthony Trollope's Archdeacon Grantly, or Joanna Trollope's parish priest from *The Rector's Wife* – all of them are fascinating because of the way in which they are compromised by their own calling.

It is the dilemma that Kenneth Mason neatly defines when he describes ministry as 'necessary but impossible, impossible but necessary'.[3] 'They are to represent humanity and represent God without falsifying the image of either, and therefore without becoming a third reality in themselves, different from both.'[4]

It is the challenge Richard Hooker described more grandly:

The power of the ministry of God translateth out of darkness into glory, it raiseth men from earth and bringeth God himself down from heaven, by blessing visible elements it maketh them invisible grace, it giveth daily the Holy Ghost, it hath to dispose of that flesh which was given for the life of the world and that blood which was poured out to redeem souls ... O wretched blindness if we admire not so great power, more wretched if we consider it aright and notwithstanding imagine that any but God can bestow it![5]

An extraordinary task required of ordinary men and women. We cannot help but notice the incongruities, the scale of expectation, and the certainty of failure.

Priests try, simultaneously, to build community and to change it. Scripture offers us a narrative in which humanity is driven out of Eden and seeks the city of God. It is a story fraught with difficulty. In the Exodus, pain and anger loom large. Again and again, in the wilderness, God's people debated the business of staying here and moving on, and argued. Moses' ministry was a constant struggle. He was dogged by questions about authority and consent.

'If only we had died by the hand of the LORD in the land of Egypt, when we sat by the fleshpots and ate our fill of bread;

for you have brought us out into this wilderness to kill this whole assembly with hunger.'[6]

These same questions of authority and consent are the fundamental experience of ministry. After McCabe described ministers as revolutionaries he pointed out that revolutionaries are not often popular (and a parish church is never going to be a natural habitat): 'I think it is significant that, according to St John, the first thing Jesus says about the missionaries he commissions before his death is that the world will hate them.' Every priest, ministering to things as they are, praying for things as they should be, will encounter questions about what authority they have to challenge us and move us on. Issues of authority and consent are the fundamental experience of a ministry that has its origin in Christ. The Gospels should alert us to that; they describe the arguments that raged around Jesus as he challenged the religious community to live up to the vocation they professed:

When he entered the temple, the chief priests and the elders of the people came to him as he was teaching, and said, 'By what authority are you doing these things, and who gave you this authority?'

They were astounded at his teaching, for he taught them as one having authority, and not as the scribes.

They were all amazed and kept saying to one another, 'What kind of utterance is this? For with authority and power he commands the unclean spirits, and out they come!'

'Father, the hour has come; glorify your Son so that the Son may glorify you, since you have given him authority over all people, to give eternal life to all whom you have given him.'[7]

We require the clergy to make it their vocation to remind us of our vocation. They can easily disappoint us by doing their work badly, but they can cause us worse distress by doing their work well. Reminding us that we should not be comfortable with the home we have made for ourselves, the clergy become a thorn in our side.

The Church and the ministry of the Church have to show us the future and invite us to go there. Somehow we have to look at the clergy and see past them. Somehow they have to make that possible. And still the questions of their authority and our consent will keep surfacing. As they become more familiar to us, as we get to know them better the questions persist. When Jesus preached salvation, one of the things that puzzled his critics was that they knew him: 'Is not this the carpenter's son? Is not his mother called Mary?'[8] This is why so many of our arguments about our shared humanity surface for a second time within the Church. We might think we have accepted the idea of equality, but when a woman or someone who is gay is ordained, and we have to consent to them, we are put to the test.

In much the same way, when we sit in a service of induction at the beginning of a new ministry and watch the slightly self-conscious procession of welcomes, we are watching a church striving to manage the business of mutual recognition and consent. Bishop and incumbent may (or may not) understand a ministry that is 'both yours and mine'. Nearby, however, there is an uncomfortable husband or wife thinking fast about precisely what this bishop meant when he welcomed them so cheerfully and said something about 'your shared ministry'. Then there are the Sunday school teachers, and the lay ministers shuffling up and down the aisle, pacing out precisely where they fit in. The rhetoric the Church uses on occasions like this is increasingly all about different gifts and God's generous grace. We make it sound permissive and cheerful. In truth, an induction service is a sharp reminder that the Church is also an ordered community in which the untidiness of extravagant grace will be arranged into very specific tasks and roles, some of which are more official than others. It is not just questions of expectation and responsibility that we have to settle – all that argument over who does what and to whom. We need to establish what gives someone the right to speak and lead in the Christian community. As the community changes, as the clumsy humanity of the priest intrudes, that conversation usually becomes more painful.

We have come a long way from Mr Dumble and his chrysanthemums. Ministry may be local and particular, but it also has to be *restless*. It can adapt itself, but it should be an agent of change. It can be official, but it should also be inspiring. There are different assumptions about what it might look like and how it might behave. Ministry strives to build community, but then turns on the community because it has drawn the wrong boundaries or fashioned a false hope. It is inevitable that ministry will be challenged. We should notice that it is often the most religious people who express the challenge. It was the Pharisees who challenged Jesus; it was the priests and court prophets who denounced Jeremiah. When ministry is at its most restless and energetic, that is when it is most disturbing, When ministry is inspired, then the feathers really begin to fly.

The *Didache*, a matter of life and death

It is that conversation, a fairly heated conversation about inspiration, that we encounter in the *Didache* (*didachē* is a Greek word, meaning 'teaching'). Scholars pause at this point and debate important questions about precisely when and where the *Didache* was written. The range of suggested dates extends from 50 to 120 CE, but the academic consensus now favours the earlier part of that period. If that is true, then the *Didache* is one of the earliest Christian texts we have outside scripture.[9]

The *Didache* is a short text. It does a lot with a few words. It begins by telling us that Christianity is 'a way of life'.[10] That does not mean that Christianity is a pattern of behaviour, in the way that being a lawyer, going to the opera and putting out the recycling might be called 'a way of life'. The *Didache* thinks in terms of a choice between being fully alive as Christ was alive, and of the alternative possibility of a life that is not really living at all. 'There are two ways, one of life and one of death, but a great difference between the two ways.'[11] So the *Didache* is cast within a set of assumptions about life and death, temptation, sin and redemption. The 'teaching' that gives the *Didache* its name is teaching about how to tell life from death. Although it reads like a series of challenges to an individual, the *Didache* takes no interest in personal salvation or personal development; it insists that holiness is worked out in community. In order to follow the way of life, we need the example and friendship of those who will show us what living that life looks like. So, church is important because it makes the life of Christ visible for us:

> My child, remember night and day him who speaks the word of God to you, and honour him as you do the Lord. For wherever the lordly rule is uttered, there is the Lord. And seek out day by day the faces of the saints, in order that you may rest upon their words. Do not long for division, but rather bring those who contend to peace.[12]

The steady stress on gathering the Church together is reason enough to make this an important text, but there is something more. The *Didache* is conscious of a problem. The Church in which it is written has two different types of ministers and there is an argument about which ministry is authentic and reliable. The *Didache* wrestles with problems of authority, inspiration and order.

This is a snapshot of the Church at a particular moment, when the itinerant ministry of apostles, moving from place to place, with dusty feet and good news, was beginning to give way to a much more stable pattern of ministers who stayed put. This is the Church in the years immediately after St Paul's ministry. Paul anticipated that local churches would appoint their own officers: the bishops and deacons mentioned in the First Letter to Timothy, the elders described in Titus. Yet Paul also described ministries inspired by the Spirit, and in 1 Corinthians 12 he refers to the 'apostles, prophets and teachers' who are not constrained by context. Paul expected to find both ministries. In the *Didache* something of Paul's confidence in a rich mix of roles has been lost. There is an almost brooding anxiety: 'For in the last days [the false prophets] and corrupters shall be multiplied, and the sheep shall be turned into wolves, and love shall be turned into hate.'[13] The *Didache* has already established that false teaching is perilous; it is 'the Way of Death' and it is to be feared and avoided. Ministry must be tested.

The *Didache*, with its commitment to telling one thing from another, goes to work with a will. It declares that itinerant apostles and prophets should stay no longer than two days in one place and even then only if there is need. When they leave they should take with them nothing but a little bread for the journey. Blown by the winds of the Spirit, these apostles speak the words of God, and they are given enormous respect; 'Let every apostle, when he cometh to you, be received as the Lord.'[14] And yet, still the *Didache* insists, they are to be tested: 'But if he remains three days, he is a false prophet ... If he asks for money, he is a false prophet.'[15]

And here there is just a little confusion. The *Didache* uses the terms 'apostle' and 'prophet' interchangeably and then apparently makes an important distinction between them. While apostles must move on, prophets appear to have a choice. They too can move on, or they can choose to settle, in which case they are to be given tithes from the wine press, the threshing floor and from the flocks. This is a watershed for the early Church. Over there, the lonely vocation of those who move on; over here, the careful duty of those who settle and build community. In truth the *Didache* seems to struggle with its own definitions. It tells us that the local church must choose officers, then adds, 'for they also render to you the service of prophets and teachers'.[16]

This is a glimpse of a time when the definition of ministry was still fluid. A shelf of learned papers has been written about what this tells us about the life of the early Church. The key to making sense of the muddle is to understand that *all* the ministry of the Church – missionaries and apostles, local elders and leaders, teachers and pastors – should have a passion and a care for what has already been given and still long for what is yet to come. All ministries serve a common purpose, all are connected. The language of the *Didache*, slipping from 'apostle' to 'prophet' and on into 'bishop' and 'deacon', assumes that each should borrow some of the character of others. Ministry in a rural village, or in a northern city, or a southern suburb, always longs to be part of the whole, wants to be fully catholic.

We make ministry safe by writing job descriptions and statements of particulars. We think that you get in first and mark out the boundaries. The *Didache*, however, makes rather a mess of clear distinctions between types of ministry. The pressing issue is always how you distinguish life from death. What the *Didache* knows is that ministry is fundamentally dangerous. Ministers can mislead, teach falsehood and stir up division. That is the way of death. The Church cannot afford the luxury of simply accepting the claims of every self-proclaimed apostle who blows into town. The *Didache* believes that real ministry demands respect, it 'comes in the name of the Lord', but there also has to be vigilance and a loathing of anything that is self-seeking or insincere. Vocation is not tested once, the Church tests it all the time.

That is not a task that can be left to an individual. The *Didache* assumes that the whole community will be able to tell truth from error: 'receive everyone who comes in the name of the Lord, and prove and know him afterward; for you shall have understanding right and left'.[17]

The Didache, notice, assumes that the gift of judgement lies with the community and not with the ministry. Apostles and prophets, bishops and deacons are important people, they are accorded huge respect, but they are not the experts on Christian living. At some point the issue of authority and consent has to be settled. That is done by the community, which has to recognize the ministry that it sets over and within it. It is the community that understands how you live out the gospel. It is the community that recognizes life and death. The community shapes its ministry as ministry shapes the community.

Charles Gore, Roland Allen and ministry in the Church

Alongside the New Testament, the *Didache* is one of the earliest glimpses we have of the ministry of the Church. It tells us that, from the beginning, ministry was beset by issues of authority and consent. The *Didache* wants us to understand that ministry is a task undertaken within the Church, it is not something done *to* the Church. That crisis passed, soon the Church stopped looking for itinerant apostles blowing into town on the wind of the spirit. In the years that followed, the cautious tone of the *Didache* was forgotten and the bishops of the early Church established an extraordinary personal authority. There were, of course, examples of lacklustre and compromised leadership, but there was also bravery in persecution, personal sanctity, deep learning and dogged determination. Little by little, priests were put on pedestals. There were voices raised in protest and bouts of anti-clericalism, but ordination had become a magisterial vocation. The best priests grabbed the imagination; the less able just grabbed us by the scruff of the neck. In the beliefs of groups like the Waldensians, the Lollards and some of the Protestant reformers there were attempts to assert the idea that ministry belongs to the whole Church, but it is only relatively recently that that argument has won a wider audience. Oddly, it took a rather aristocratic voice to help shift the emphasis.

Charles Gore had an uncle who was an earl. Authoritarian and rather old fashioned, Gore gave away more than he perhaps realized about his background and style when he defended his habits of reverence by declaring, 'I have genuflected since I wore black velvet breeches and I shall genuflect until I die.'[18] Yet he was also, instinctively, a radical, a champion of women's suffrage and Welsh disestablishment, as well as President of the Christian Social Union. An unconventional thinker, his ideology pulled him one way and his inheritance pulled him another. Gore was a radical out of the drawing room. His book *The Church and the Ministry* was an assault on clerical privilege, but still contained a fair amount of talk about 'above' and 'below'. It provided an informed and fairly detailed account of what St Paul and the patristic writers have to say about ecclesiology, and viewed their work through an Anglo-Catholic lens. He referred to the ordained ministry as the 'stewardship of Christian mysteries' and set it in stone. Gore believed ministry was instituted by Christ, mediated through the apostles and has been exercised continuously ever since; it came from 'above'. He wrote about the 'title deeds' of the church.[19] That was tendentious and Gore knew it. There is plenty of scholarship to suggest that Christ did not envisage the ministry of bishops, priests and area deans. Yet for all that pugnacity, his book was more subtle than it first appeared. Gore saw things whole, put them in context. He knew that ministry belongs to the Church. He understood ordination to be a social act:

> [M]an is by his very essence 'a social animal'. By isolating himself he hinders, he narrows himself, he perishes: by merging himself in the larger whole, he realizes his true individuality and his true freedom. So when God sent redemption upon the earth, He sent it in a community or kingdom. Fellowship with God is to be won through fellowship with His Son, but that not otherwise than through fellowship with His Church.[20]

Gore believed that there cannot possibly be anything to add to the incarnation, the gospel or the work of the Spirit. So, the Church lacks nothing; it has 'a finality which belongs to its very essence'.[21] Together the members of the Christian community have all the resources they need. The Church as a whole is a royal priesthood, a holy nation. Although Gore used the Fathers (at length) to prove to his own satisfaction that the ordained ministry comes from the 'title deeds', he employed them first to show that there is a common priesthood that belongs to all Christians.

That left him to explain just what ministry was proper for those who are ordained. Gore thought that the life of the Church was rich and various and expressed by different people in different ways. Certain tasks had been set aside, by Christ, for particular people.

[T]he ministry is the organ, the necessary organ of these functions. It is the hand which offers and distributes; it is the voice which consecrates and pleads. And the whole body can no more dispense with its services than the natural body can grasp or speak without the instrumentality of hand and tongue. Thus the ministry is the instrument as well as the symbol of the Church's unity, and no man can share her fellowship except in acceptance of its offices.[22]

So the clergy are important, but only as important as the particular role they have in the life of the body of Christ. It is the body that is pre-eminent. They are servants of the whole and instruments of God's purpose. Even as they engage in the crucial task of sustaining unity, they must acknowledge that work of grace goes ahead of them. Religion is God's gift to the Church; it is not something that the ministry creates.

Christianity is the life of an organized society ... [the clergy] are the instrument of unity ... But the individual life can receive this fellowship with God only through membership in the one body and by dependence upon social sacraments of regeneration, of confirmation, of communion, of absolution, of which ordained ministers are the appointed instruments. A fundamental principle of Christianity is that of social dependence.[23]

Gore insisted that ministry is worked out in the church community, a conclusion the *Didache* came to by another route. The weakness in Gore's argument was his insistence on the 'finality' of the Church. The point he was making, of course, is that there is no further revelation to come: scripture and tradition are all the blessing and grace we need. The trouble is that, once you have said that we already are what we shall be, you can come to believe that all you need to do is to administer a tweak here and rely on a bit of wise episcopal leadership there, and all manner of things will be well. Gore, aristocrat and bishop, was perhaps always going to struggle to imagine that the arrival of the Kingdom might overturn the tea things. His was the radical voice speaking from *within* the synods and councils of the Church. He could not perhaps quite imagine what ministry might need to become if it was truly the instrument of regeneration. Others, equally committed to the ministry of the whole people of God, would be less certain that ordained ministry was quite the given that Gore claimed and would ask, instead, what different ministry the Church might actually need.

In 1930 Roland Allen published *The Case for Voluntary Clergy*. It was a passionate, even an angry, book. Allen thought of himself as a voice crying in the wilderness (and thus neatly subverted awkward questions about his own limited experience – prophets are not accountable). He rather wryly observed:

> I never ask anyone to do anything, and consequently I do not get a 'yes' or a 'no'. I say what seems to be obviously true, but they do not know what to do about it. One day someone will see what action is demanded, and perhaps screw up their courage to take it. If I were out to organize and lead that would be different, but as you well know I long ago decided that was not the way of the Spirit for me.[24]

It is the phrase 'the way of the Spirit' that is the key to making any sense of this extraordinary man. It was not just that he had a developed theology of the work of the Spirit (though that was certainly true); the work of the Spirit was a fact of life for Allen. The Spirit made him maverick. Ordained to a title parish in Darlington, his real vocation was always to the mission field, and in 1895 the Society for the Propagation of the Gospel sent him to North China. He stayed there (with periods of leave) until his health broke down in 1903. For the rest of his life, however, his passion for mission drove him on long, restless journeys. Eager, opinionated and busy, he was dismissive of any attempt to measure his achievements or weigh up his work. *His* work was never the issue. Ministry is the work of 'Christ and his Apostles'; it is driven forward by the Spirit, and God alone can judge its worth.

Suspicious of process and intellect, Allen wanted the Spirit to be the 'one and only guide', to overcome all doubt as to what was the mind of God.[25] It is a powerful argument, but it takes no prisoners. Restless and critical, he could not settle in parish ministry and struggled to work with others. *The Case for Voluntary Clergy* draws a stark contrast between the 'freedom and power' of the apostles and the cautious quest for a 'plausible policy' that dominates the life of the contemporary Church.[26] In particular, it was the Church's insistence on stipendiary ministry that Allen attacked. He was prepared to acknowledge that, in certain times and in certain places, it was a system that had some merit, but at other times, for example when mission was called for, it was actually a hindrance. Refusing to allow clergy to earn a living by some other means, the Church was, he claimed, at odds with the will of Christ; it had ignored the teaching and practice of the apostles and bound itself in chains.

Allen pointed out that scripture looks for moral and social qualities in those who are going to be ordained. Bishops might want qualifications, but the New Testament wants someone who can welcome people into their home, and bring up children in a way that others admire.[27] He looked around and saw candidates for ordination offering themselves before ever the Church had called them (a phenomenon that had scandalized Gregory Nazianzus long years ago[28]) and he despaired:

we must think first and foremost of the group as the church in the place, and of the ministers as naturally and normally members of that group, attached to it by every tie, spiritual and social.[29]

The argument was urgent, impassioned and reckless, but the force behind it was an abiding assumption that ministry exists to serve the Church, not itself. Allen began with the question, 'What ministry does the Church need?' He threw down, all over again, the challenge that the *Didache* had once addressed. It is the challenge of ministries that are local set against the claims of a ministry with qualifications that no one particular community can confer. He begged questions about authority, he railed against constraint. A ministry that serves the Church, a ministry that must answer to the Church, is a ministry that must change as the Church changes.

Robin Greenwood: 'Who put the status in the status quo?'

When Eamon Duffy noted the contrast between medieval priests, who came in from the fields with mud on their hands, and the Tridentine clergy, pale from years in oratories and universities, who succeeded them, he went on to observe:

> The Tridentine moment is passing, perhaps has already passed. The sort of expertise the Tridentine priest was expected to have is now within reach of us all, and in the West we do not need or at any rate no longer want the sort of clerical guru which Trent set itself to produce. As society changes the Church calls on all the laity to claim and exercise their priesthood.[30]

This is not a change of mood; it is a change of culture and practice. Catholics and Anglicans are newly serious about our common baptism and the ministry of all believers. We are revising theology and practice and we are directing a significant amount of our resources into new forms of collaborative ministry. Over the last 20 years Robin Greenwood has been the most articulate and passionate champion of that change. The *Didache* faced a pressing challenge; Greenwood feels another:

> The Church that mostly now fails to refresh the inner parts mercifully has no future. Something new is called for if we're up for it. Abandoning defensiveness, considering what are acceptable insights and hopes among people generally, using every imaginative muscle in conversation with God ...[31]

He has a corner to fight and an axe to grind. He believes the Church is in crisis and that *local ministry*, that is, ministry *of* the community *for* the community, is the answer we need:

[A]nonymous churches that don't really mind whether you're there or not, except to boost numbers and finances, and that basically rely on the ordained minister and a band of loyal helpers are not likely to be around for very much longer. The Local Ministry spirit dances with those in every generation who have looked for a Christian community where everyone recognizes their personal and corporate invitation – as one of the Desert Fathers suggested – to be a pillar of fire.[32]

The reference to the Desert Fathers is significant. Robin Greenwood's books are a heady cocktail of authorities, theologians, physicists, social theorists, anthropologists and therapists jostling for attention and forcing the pace of a different kind of theological enquiry. In all this, one theological preference is unquestionably dominant. Greenwood believes that trinitarian doctrine is the proper and only foundation for thinking about the life of the Church.

At the very heart of the trinitarian God, he says, is communion. God is authority and obedience without hierarchy. We can share that life when we too live in relationship. It sounds uncontroversial, but it is actually a body blow to the old, presiding conversation about ministry. We usually assume that it is in our *individuality* that we are related to God. We talk about our particular, individual gifts; we keep journals and describe our experience. We ask for 'personal inventories' when we discern vocation. Spirituality and faith are routinely linked to the enneagram and to Myers Briggs personality types (and convince us we can speak of 'my ministry'). Greenwood is much more interested in community than individuality. Worse still, in Greenwood's eyes, we are obsessed with status and power. He is convinced the Church has failed to take seriously the communion that is the life of God: 'The prevailing ministerial patterns of the contemporary Church reveal few connections with the inter-relatedness of God, of people and the entire cosmos.'[33]

He urges us to accept the idea that it is the job of the Church to lead us into maturity, into the kind of relationship that is the very life of God. Knowing about the Trinity, everything 'looks different'. He makes sure we do not miss the point:

I have reached three important conclusions ... First, God's being is most accurately understood by Christians as Trinity: a communion of Father, Son and Holy Spirit. Second, it is essential to God's purpose for the universe that all relationships should be understood as echoing the trinitarian pattern. Third, the Church, having a particular task to prepare the way for godly relationships in society and creation, must allow its ministerial arrangements to echo the trinitarian relationships of loving communion.[34]

The tone is theologically informed and urgent. Greenwood believes that we must make a new commitment to a properly understood theology of church. What holds us back is our competitiveness; he finds us obsessed with the language of hierarchy and subordination. Ministry must be communion, a common enterprise.

We need the confidence to recognize the disabling power of a culture of restrictive hierarchical power. It brings with it blame, and a fear of shifts in understanding God ... Almost unspeakable is the hard reality that between members and leaders of Christian communities there is not only love, respect and affection, but also misunderstanding, competitive ambition, polarized desires for the Church's future, jealousy, envy and even hostility.[35]

Part of the attraction trinitarian doctrine holds for him is that in a communion of mutual love there are no hierarchies.

Greenwood's numerous books are a siege engine against inherited forms of church. He is an enthusiast for something else, something more various. He is excited by plurality, difference and miscellany. That helps explain why so many of his metaphors are about weaving, or dancing.

I find some of the greatest clues for a Church's identity now in a rich mixture of worship, order and spontaneity; wrestling with life of many boundaries; entering into creative, joyful power; weaving emotion with intellect; manifesting commitment to those on the edge of society and Church.[36]

These are the sort of words that make archdeacons look thoughtful. Spontaneity never used to be a particularly Anglican virtue; it was never looked for in visitation articles. Greenwood is undeterred; he believes that it is high time we had a different culture, high time the local church freed itself from bondage.[37]

He has confidence in each local community and this is ground that the *Didache* treads. Greenwood, it should be said, has a rather more radical edge. So, for example, it is a commonplace to suggest that the Church is apostolic when it is continuous from generation to generation.[38] Greenwood dismisses the idea that apostolicity might have something to do with our hold on the past. You see real apostolicity, he argues, when individuals imitate the apostles and long for the Kingdom.[39] The clergy will have to work out new roles in this dispensation. In his most recent writing, there is an increasing stress on ministry understood as a 'reckless and hopeful' task and on vulnerability as a necessary quality in the clergy.[40] He turns priests into navigators, helping the community discern a sense of direction.[41] The clergy will prompt the community into reflection; they will be people of 'discernment' and they will be 'witnesses', a bridge between congregation and all creation. These are ideas that are newly welcome. The liberation of the ministry of the whole people of God has made huge progress in recent years. We are recovering the conviction that bustles through the pages of the First letter to the Corinthians, or *1 Clement*, that we are all gifted and that ministry is various. There is no one model of holiness and we no longer want to sit under experts.

Even so, Greenwood thinks that there are forces of opposition mustered against what he says. He tells us that advocates of change are 'punished or left in the cold'.[42] He has individuals in mind; there is also a natural caution that inhibits us. With one hand we beckon forward the ministry of the whole people of God, and with the other we indicate that they should not move so fast. He is right: expertise and professional competence are always exclusive. Just as we overcome one set of assumptions, our anxieties about safeguarding, health and safety and conditions of service create new hierarchies. We offer courses in youth work and find that volunteers feel disempowered and anxious. We ask for volunteers and then weigh them down with handbooks. We step back to defer to people with skills and, instead of liberating every-member ministry, we just create a new cadre of people with badges and titles. Deeply concerned about numbers and money, dioceses work harder to be seen to be efficient and produce spreadsheets full of measurable outcomes. The hierarchy changes as 'strategy delivery' makes servants of us all.

We struggle to do as Greenwood asks because we keep reverting to type and, for all our delight in community, we have developed a taste for celebrity (we really learnt nothing from the *Didache*). We want leaders and symbols of success a little more than is good for us. We talk about joyful spontaneity, but find it tiring and unpredictable and we shuffle back to cautious communities where we all know what to expect. And there is still one more difficulty. There is a glimpse of the trouble that might be in store in what Greenwood has to say about 'membership'. Determined to build community, he needs to define what that community might be and so he starts to talk of 'members'. It is not a term that the gospel employs; there are no 'members' of the Kingdom, it never has been a club you can join. Membership is seductive; it clothes itself in privilege and identity. Even local ministry teams can occasionally become less generous than they intend. When the vicar joins the team we abandon presidential rule and install government by cabinet instead. Greenwood understands the problem. His understanding of community is generous; the people who come after him do not all have those instincts. Barricades are overthrown and neat new fences go up.

There is a paradox at work when we start to think about ministry. Ministry exists to serve the Church; the call to ministry is a call to abandon dreams of status: 'the greatest among you must become like the youngest, and the leader like one who serves'.[43] Yet, when we write about ministry, or plan for it, we set it about with definitions. We make it special and, to our intense surprise, it acquires status. When we acknowledge the problem and talk about the vocation we share in baptism, we lose our grip on the definitions and struggle to assign the tasks of mission and the responsibilities of worship. The truth is that relationships are difficult and go on being difficult. It is the nature of the Church to be a community that wrestles with competition and issues of status. Greenwood longs for the Church to know God in Trinity and to know itself in that same communion The problem is that the Trinity is not, in the end, the way we know God. The Trinity is the way *God* knows God. When Augustine wrote about the Trinity he was careful to remind us that we were trespassing where we had little right to be:

> [W]hen the question is asked, What three? human language labours altogether under great poverty of speech. The answer, however, is given, three persons, not that it might be [completely] spoken, but that it might not be left [wholly] unspoken.[44]

The Trinity is the profoundly mysterious business of the way God relates to himself and to his action. We do not *know* God in Trinity; we know God because he revealed himself in Christ. Our first responsibility is to follow Christ (it is what he told us to do). The Church is not an expression of the life of the Trinity; it is the body of Christ. Our identity is secured in baptism not because it is the sacrament of relationship, but because it is there that we die to self and rise with Christ. Christian vocation and all the ministries that flow from it might be worked out in relationship, but they take their fundamental character from the call of Christ. Of course, our destiny is the Kingdom where we will live in community. Of course, we are called to be Christ's body *together*, and of course we must be ambitious for shared ministry and full communion. Even so, we do not have a vocation to be part of a ministry team; we have a vocation to follow Christ into the world and to live his life in our own time. Following Christ, we are constantly dying to self, constantly ridding ourselves of competition and the obsession with status. The Church here on earth is a work in progress, the theatre of grace. In that Church, servants are given specific tasks to perform; ordination helps provide order and we argue out our route to the Kingdom. Robin Greenwood is right, the servants do keep becoming the masters, and the Church is dying in good order. It is deeply depressing that we have read St Paul, encountered a carnival of gifts and come away with just one thing to say about vocation – that you can be, or can't be, a priest. Acknowledging that mistake, however, we must not make another and force everyone into a team, or abandon the catholic for the local.

The *Didache* noted that itinerant apostles and prophets were getting too self-important and reminded the Church that a local community had wisdom and authority. Greenwood shares that confidence in the local community, but there are no apostles now and parishes have started to talk about 'the diocese' as though it was someone else, somewhere else with questionable motives. The local dialect is rapidly becoming the only language that we trust, and any mildly itinerant minister (bishops included) will tell you that the variety in practice, worship and belief is now bewildering. Ever alert, Greenwood's more recent work includes a responsibility to remind the Church of its catholic vocation.[45] He also speaks with renewed passion about longing for full humanity in Christ.[46] He knows as well as any of us that escaping one constraint we easily invent new hierarchies to make ourselves feel safe.

A woman's place is at the altar

In 1993, John Major, then the Prime Minister, told us that some things about England would not change. With a rather uncharacteristic, rhetorical flourish he looked 50 years into the future and saw an England that was still the country of 'long shadows on cricket grounds, warm beer, invincible green suburbs, dog lovers and pools fillers'. It was a passionate attempt to identify the hallmarks of our life, the things that define. There is a kind of party game to be played here; a dinner party conversation about the symbols that define us. It is a game the Church has played: hassocks and cassocks, *Hymns Ancient and Modern* (spotted with mildew), church flowers, the parish magazine (two months out of date) and lichen on a gravestone.

These stories do not work any longer. John Major was fighting a corner and he was losing, his vision of England was quickly derided. Warm beer is all very well, but where were the young men and women swigging Bacardi Breezers in pedestrian precincts? Where were the bottles of Krug for bankers on bonuses? We are rightly suspicious of these agreed narratives now. The presiding image of parish Anglicanism is not the Book of Common Prayer, but the rota that tells you that, this week, the Eucharist you are looking for is in another village at 9.30 (unless, of course, it is the fifth Sunday in the month). Not very long ago I strode up a church path on a Sunday, clutching my alb, to find the door locked. A few minutes scouting around and I discovered I had come to Whittington and should have been in Withington, five miles away (where a churchwarden was being handed the radio microphone because the stupid priest had not yet appeared). It is hard to belong when you do not know where you should be.

John Major's famous (or infamous) speech was not just conservative with a small 'c', it was a study in unexamined prejudice, as much about our *not* being Europeans as it was about the glory of being English. It was a rhetoric that looked backwards, lagged behind the experience it tried to describe. That is what happens when we negotiate change. The discourse struggles to keep up. In the Church of England our theological discourse is constantly several paces behind local experience. We are always debating ministry because ministry is always contentious and public doctrine lags behind worked experience. Our ecclesiology is done on the hoof.

So, to offer the obvious example, the controlling narrative about ministry is undeniably masculine. The authors cited in this book were men writing (at least until very recently) for men. What they have said has been a blessing to the Church, but it can also be felt as a burden or a constraint. When Bridget Macaulay was finally ordained after a long period of testing her vocation to priesthood she became a curate in Edinburgh. Struggling in a long, heavy cope (made for a man) through evensong and benediction, she reflected:

It felt like I was carrying this mantle of tradition of a male priesthood that has been with us for centuries, and it's a beautiful thing. A beautiful, ornate and rich thing – so this is not knocking what has been – but I got up to the front where there is the really good, strong, *male* choir. I'm not knocking that either, its beautiful. But I'm not confident about singing in church, and I heard this little girl's reedy voice coming out of my mouth ... I was nearly overwhelmed by the feeling that women's priesthood is like being a little girl in a sea of grown men.[47]

What Bridget Macaulay manages to do here, with grace and generosity, is to acknowledge that the inheritance that comes with priesthood can be attractive and rich without necessarily being a good fit. Others are not so sure. Marilyn McCord Adams prefers to name and shame a deep tradition of sinful misogyny in the Church. She identifies an inheritance that simply needs to be destroyed.[48]

The ordination of women, the consecration of women bishops, the experience of women in the Church are all significant illustrations of a ministry that changes and of a theology that adapts. There are continuities, crucial continuities. Women are now ordained into the historic ordained ministry of the Church. That ministry is conferred by the same authority, sustained by the same grace and governed by the same canons that it always was. There are discontinuities too. Women have been forced to turn a kind of somersault in dealing first with the experience of being denied the possibility of ordination and then, in short order, being welcomed and asked why more of them were not candidates for preferment. Janet Fife has written about learning to think differently:

Long ago I learned to find God in my experience of being silenced and of rejection. For me the most meaningful day in the church year was Good Friday. Now I am learning to find God in the experience of being heard and respected ... perhaps it is no coincidence that I now lead the Church of the Resurrection.[49]

Margaret Webster suggests that it is as if we had 'walked through a looking glass'.[50] As long ago as 1984, Ursula King looked back on a changing consciousness and looked forward to something new:

> [O]ver the last twenty years women have spoken out with ever increasing strength and entered into a new dialogue. They have discovered themselves and each other, they have learnt to perceive and criticize the deep injustices done to them and they have developed an amazing ability to envisage alternatives.[51]

That business of envisaging alternatives is the key. It is the challenge of not being defined by the moment, not being constrained by the particular. The ordained ministry is one way in which human beings follow in the footsteps of Christ. Before it is anything else, before it is preaching, or teaching, or pastoral work, or counselling, ministry is a way of life, a striving to be human as Christ was human. The hallmark of that ministry has to be a humanity that we can share. When too much rests on the fact that I am male, or white, or married (or a bit introverted and given to reading poetry and drinking claret), then ministry is impoverished. My particularity is what makes me interesting, or infuriating, to others and will always colour my ministry, but the peculiar calling of the clergy is to describe, for others, a life we can share.

Ordained ministry is awkward, controversial and human. It keeps getting snagged on the wrong sort of particularity. It has certainly been far too masculine and it has been impoverished as a result. Yet we will miss the point if we go on speaking of a male or female ministry, or become fascinated with 'straight' and 'gay' ministry. That suggests that there is something *particular* in Christ's humanity that we must seek out, a subset of being humanity that matters most. Down that road lies a terrible error needing Christ to be like me, when in truth it is me that needs to be more like Christ. We need to stumble over the statistics and notice that ministry is too narow and too particular. Statistics, however will not offer us a solution. We do not need a working party to suggest that next year 52 per cent of our ordinands must be women and 48 per cent male, 33 per cent BME, 60 per cent extrovert, and 2 per cent mystical. We do need to ordain clergy who are all wholly committed to Christ's generous humanity. We do need clergy who in their glorious, infuriating diversity and peculiarity can help us see past them to a Kingdom that we can share.

Writing about the ordination of women, ten years after the historic vote in General Synod, Rowan Williams was clear that thanks to the glorious, gracious, God-given ministry of women we understand better that we minister differently, *perform* differently.

> The moment of significant newness in the Church's history, language and practice needs to be understood as an uncovering of connections and resonances in our central doctrines that have never before been 'brought out in performance', as we might say. The analogy is serious: a good, new Shakespearian production may shake us up in its unconventionality, but if it is really good it will make us say, 'I never saw that', so that we go away from the theatre not thinking about a new and different play, but ready to read and ponder in a way that shows new depths in what we thought was familiar.[52]

Rowan Williams shifts the debate. The Church does not look to its priests for a glimpse of real Christian discipleship. It is a calamity for the Church that our fixation on ordination has hijacked our idea of what committed discipleship looks like. Priests do not define Christian identity, Christ does that in baptism. Priests call the community of the baptized to be what it should be, to live up to its calling. It is baptism, not ordination, that fixes our identity. In baptism each one of us resigns the right to see what we can make of ourselves, in order to discover what we might become in Christ. It is baptism that says interesting things about us and it is baptism that should be the focus of our concern. Rowan Williams writes:

What we should be looking for and praying for is the revived commitment to what the identity in Christ of the baptised is all about, only then can the ordained do their distinctive job of telling and showing the Church what it is.[53]

Putting priests in their place

The drama and public performance of particular styles of ministry always threatens to overwhelm the community. Ministry is supposed to build up our common life; as Rowan Williams has argued, it needs to 'get out of the way'. We still need to learn how to celebrate our common baptism and abandon our fixation that real Christian vocation must lead to ordination. The Church is significantly the poorer twice over. Poorer because we do not have anything approaching a serious theology of Christian vocation. Poorer, too, because we trust the local church to deliver diversity for us. Uncertain about catholic order, we now have an occasionally chaotic enthusiasm for local solutions; little by little it will turn us congregational and parochial.

Working out what it means for each of us to follow Christ and eager to celebrate our human diversity, embraced and reconciled in Christ, churches have gradually grown more generous in their understanding of ministry. At the boundaries of that generosity, though, we still have our most bitter arguments. Those arguments are inevitable; we have always had them, we always will. We have to have the arguments. They are not about religious housekeeping and who is allowed to do what; they are arguments about what we think humanity looks like. We will continue to argue about what kinds of human diversity we will tolerate standing at our altars and in our pulpits. Meanwhile, a church growing more comfortable with variety finds it stands a little looser to a shared inheritance, and our unity consequently becomes more fragile. Practice and culture vary from parish to parish. It is still, however, peculiarly, the vocation of the clergy to summon the community of God's people from the settlements they have made into the

Kingdom that is to come. The challenge that the *Didache* negotiated takes a different guise. Ministers make a commitment to
a place and a people, and celebrate the life they find there. The
rewards are great, but we find we are less comfortable when we
gather in greater congregations at ordinations or synods.

Clement of Alexandria explained, long ago, that the Church
is meant to be a glimpse of the future: 'Just as God's will is
creation and is called the world so his intention is the salvation
of men and it is called the church.'[54] We need a clergy who can
share some common vision, some common understanding for
a future we will all share. The clergy themselves need to have
learnt that language that they can offer to us and one another,
before they encounter the experiences that will pull them apart.

In the *Didache*, and in the works of Gore, Allen and Greenwood, we have seen that ministry does not govern the Church.
The Church calls and the Church deploys, setting the agenda
for ministry. It is the clergy themselves that have to work out
what calling and intention actually add up to in a particular
place, but they do that in response to the primary action of
God in the Church It is a point again explained by Rowan
Williams:

> [T]he Church is first of all a kind of space cleared by God
> through Jesus in which people may become what God made
> them to be (God's sons and daughters), and that what we have
> to do about the Church is not first to organise it as a society
> but to inhabit it as a climate or a landscape. It is a place where
> we can see properly – God, God's creation, ourselves.[55]

The language of leadership, which we use so often, must not
mask the fundamental truth that the Church is the theatre of
God's action and that ministry is always a response to God's
grace. There is nothing wrong with leadership – we need leadership. We need leadership that is the servant, not the master, of
the gospel; we need leadership that points away from itself,
and we really need a leadership that knows that it belongs in
community and depends on grace. The call is not to be busy, it
is not even to be *effective*. Gnosticism is not the threat it was

(even though it is alive and well); our error lies elsewhere. Now we could all too easily become a Pelagian church in which we believe it is up to us to solve all our problems. Pelagianism makes life a project in which the watchword is 'improvement'. That is the temptation in leadership, the temptation to be 'in charge'. At a very simple level it is a temptation that frustrates collegiality and interdependence. In a church it does something worse, it sets goals and measures successes that are always less than the real scale of our hope. It points to what can be done and not to the Kingdom of God that is yet to come. It turns back to the plough; it buries the dead. Ministry is service not achievement. The *Didache*, one of the earliest texts on ministry, makes the point that must be made: ministry, or priesthood, takes its character from God's action in the Church.

Notes

1 A. N. Wilson, *Unguarded Hours*, London: Hamlyn, 1983, p. 139.

2 H. McCabe, *Law, Language and Love*, London: Sheed & Ward, 1968, pp. 151–2.

3 K. Mason, *Priesthood and Society*, Norwich: Canterbury Press, 2002, p. 11.

4 Mason, *Priesthood and Society*, p. 13.

5 R. Hooker, *Of the Laws of Ecclesiastical Polity*, in J. Keble (ed.), *The Works*, Oxford: The Clarendon Press, 1865, II, p. 166.

6 Exodus 16.2.

7 Matthew 21.23; Mark 1.22; Luke 4.36; John 17.1–2.

8 Matthew 13.55.

9 On the *Didache*, see T. O'Loughlin, *The Didache: A Window on the Earliest Christians*, London: Baker Academic, 2010; K. Niederwimmer, *The Didache: A Commentary*, trans. L. M. Maloney, ed. H. W. Attridge, Hermeneia Series, Minneapolis, MN: Fortress Press, 1998; J. A. Draper, 'The Apostolic Fathers: The *Didache*', *The Expository Times*, vol. 117, no. 5 (2006), pp. 177–81.

10 *Didache* 1, trans. A. Roberts and J. Donaldson, http://www.earlychristianwritings.com/text/didache-roberts.html.

11 *Didache* 1.

12 *Didache* 4.

13 *Didache* 16.6.

14 *Didache* 11.5.

15 *Didache* 11.

16 *Didache* 15.

17 *Didache* 12.

18 A. Hastings, *A History of English Christianity 1920–1985*, London: Collins, 1986, p. 80.

19 C. Gore, *The Church and the Ministry*, London: SPCK, 1949, p. 1.

20 Gore, *The Church and the Ministry*, pp. 43, 44.

21 Gore, *The Church and the Ministry*, p. 54

22 Gore, *The Church and the Ministry*, pp. 72, 73.

23 Gore, *The Church and the Ministry*, p. 79.

24 R. Allen, *Pentecost and the World: The Revelation of the Holy Spirit in the 'Acts of the Apostles'* (London: Oxford University Press, 1917), in R. Allen, *The Ministry of the Spirit: Selected Writings of Roland Allen*, ed. D. M. Paton, Cambridge: Lutterworth Press, 2006, p. xxv.

25 Allen, *Pentecost and the World*, in *The Ministry of the Spirit*, p. 45.

26 R. Allen, *The Case for Voluntary Clergy* (London: Eyre and Spottiswoode, 1930), in *The Ministry of the Spirit*, p. 137. It should be noted that this is a much edited version of the original text.

27 1 Timothy 3.4–5; Titus 1.8.

28 Gregory Nazianzus, *Oration*, 2.8, trans. C. G. Brown and J. E. Swallow, *N&PNF* 2S, 7.

29 Allen, *The Case for Voluntary Clergy*, in *The Ministry of the Spirit*, p. 146.

30 E. Duffy, *Faith of Our Fathers: Reflections on Catholic Tradition*, London: Continuum, 2004, p. 106.

31 R. Greenwood, *Transforming Church: Liberating Structures for Ministry*, London: SPCK, 2002, p. 92.

32 Greenwood, *Transforming Church*, p. 79.

33 R. Greenwood, *Parish Priests: For the Sake of the Kingdom*, London: SPCK, 2009, p. 13.

34 Greenwood, *Transforming Church*, p. 87.

35 Greenwood, *Transforming Church*, p. 38.

36 Greenwood, *Transforming Church*, p. 23.

37 Greenwood, *Transforming Priesthood*, London: SPCK, 1994, p. 134.

38 Doctrine Commission, *Doctrine in the Church of England* (1922), cited in G. R. Evans and J. R. Wright (eds), *The Anglican Tradition: A Handbook of Sources*, London: SPCK, 1991, p. 410.

39 See Greenwood, *Transforming Priesthood*, pp. 136–7, and Greenwood, *Parish Priests*, pp. 74–5.

40 R. Greenwood, *Being Church: The Formation of Christian Community*, London: SPCK, 2013, pp. 56–9, 171.

41 Greenwood, *Parish Priests*, p. 154.

42 Greenwood, *Transforming Church*, p. 3.

43 Luke 22.26.

44 Augustine, *On the Trinity*, V.9, trans. A. W. Haddan, *N&PNF* 1S, 3.

45 Greenwood, *Parish Priests*, p.124.

46 Greenwood, *Parish Priests*, p. 119.

47 B. Macaulay, 'Job-Sharing the Priesthood', in L. Barr and A. Barr, (eds), *Jobs for the Boys? Women who became Priests*, London: Hodder & Stoughton, 2001, p. 219.

48 M. McCord Adams, 'Afterword', in H. Harris and J. Shaw (eds), *The Call for Women Bishops*, London: SPCK, 2004, pp. 193–6.

49 J. Fife,' Unlearning and Relearning Leadership', in C. Rees (ed.), *Voices of this Calling*, Norwich: Canterbury Press, 2002, p. 107.

50 M. Webster, *A New Strength, A New Song*, London: Mowbray, 1994, p. 190.

51 U. King, 'Women in Dialogue: A New Vision of Ecumenism', *Heythrop Journal*, no. 26, quoted in Webster, *A New Strength, A New Song*, p.139. For other views, see also M. Tanner, 'Christian Feminism: A Challenge to the Churches', Loughborough University Chaplaincy Annual Lecture, 1986, quoted in Webster, *A New Strength, A New Song*, p. 140; and S. Durber, *Preaching Like a Woman*, London: SPCK, 2007, p. 1.

52 R. Williams, 'Epilogue', in Rees (ed.), *Voices of this Calling*, p. 213.

53 Williams, 'Epilogue', p. 214.

54 Clement, *The Instructor*, I.6, ANF, 2, and cited in *The Catechism of the Catholic Church*, Part One, Section 2, 3.760, http://www.vatican. va/archive/ENG0015/_INDEX.HTM.

55 From a lecture, 'The Christian Priest Today', at Ripon College, Cuddesdon, http://rowanwilliams.archbishopofcanterbury.org/articles. php/2097/the-christian-priest-today-lecture-on-the-occasion-of-the-150th-anniversary-of-ripon-college-cuddesd#sthash.mT4qJTKy.dpuf.

6

Ministers of the Kingdom

A countrey parson?

Holiness is *distinctiveness*; it is what the word means. Something holy is 'different', it is 'set apart'. We have to turn aside to find holy places; holy people do things differently. Thomas Aquinas thought that holiness was both a form of separation and that it had a particular quality, a form of dedication, that he called 'firmness'.[1] Real holiness sets a person apart and has the resilience to sustain that separation. In the story from the Desert Fathers, which gave a book title to Rowan Williams, two very different, but very holy men are pictured in 'two large boats floating on the river ... In one of them sat Abba Arsenius and the Holy Spirit of God in complete silence. And in the other boat was Abba Moses, with the angels of God: they were all eating honey cakes.'[2] Rowan Williams uses the story to illustrate the important fact that holiness takes different forms, but we need to notice too, that the image of boats on a river sets the two men a little apart from us and even from each other.

The trouble is that holiness is an awkward virtue. We struggle with particularity and peculiarity, they make us uncomfortable, and writers who explore that theme provoke strong reactions in us. The strongest reactions gather around the most particular voices. That is why so many arguments swirl around the ministry of George Herbert. A priest who is one of the truly great poets, and a scholar, and courtier living in rural seclusion, is always going to be a difficult man to place. Herbert is contested ground; his story is always being revised, or buffed and burnished until he almost disappears from view. There are claims and counter claims about his churchmanship, and what he really *means*. There are worshippers at the shrine and those who rise up and deride 'the myth of the Country Parson'.[3]

The familiar biography records that George Herbert was born in April 1593, the grandson of Sir Edward Herbert. He came from privilege, and its associations never left him; his cousins were the Earls of Pembroke. Educated at Westminster School and Trinity College, Cambridge, he was set for a career at court. George Herbert, however, began to buy theological books, because he was 'setting foot into Divinity, to lay the platform of my future life'. Ordained deacon in July 1626, the benefits of his previous life secured him a prebendal stall at Lincoln Cathedral and the living of Leighton Bromswold in Huntingdonshire. In truth, these duties did not much interfere with his life as a member of a blue-blooded family. He was required only to preach an annual sermon at Lincoln (and even then a deputy could do it for him). The church at Leighton Bromswold, meanwhile, was a ruin, which Herbert set about restoring, though quite possibly without ever visiting it in person. The decisive move came later, in April 1630, when he was instituted as Rector of Fugglestone-with-Bemerton (then two separate villages, now a western suburb of Salisbury). He settled in Bemerton and worked as a parish priest until consumption killed him just three years later.

Herbert had begun writing poetry at Cambridge, but the responsibility of parochial ministry prompted him to write a book that was, for generations, *the* classic textbook on ministry. *A PRIEST to the TEMPLE, or The Countrey Parson HIS CHARACTER AND Rule of Holy Life* is an awkward book. It was always an awkward book, only published after Herbert's death; it was first sold at a time when Anglican ministry was illegal. The difficulty goes deeper than that, it is a difficulty of tone. Herbert's motive in writing *The Countrey Parson* is explained in the Preface, 'The Authour to the Reader':

> I have resolved to set down the Form and Character of a true Pastour, that I may have a Mark to aim at: which also I will set as high as I can, since hee shoots higher that threatens the Moon, then hee that aims at a Tree.[4]

This is considered prose and it needs taking seriously. We should take note that Herbert was writing for himself ('considering with myself' was how he described it). We will also misunderstand him completely if we fail to observe that he was setting out a counsel of perfection, 'a Mark to aim at'. His book was a very particular type of literature, popular at the time, in which the stress fell on aspiration. Critics berate Herbert because he idealized ministry and made a rod for the vicar's back, but *The Countrey Parson* was never a practical handbook. To make any sense of this little book we must first understand that it was written out of a theological conviction that we are summoned by grace and we will fall short. Herbert did set an ideal, but he knew how to fail. Pick up his poems and there is no mistaking the fact that he always depended on grace, not effort.

> Blessings beforehand, tyes of gratefulnesse,
>   The sound of glorie ringing in our eares;
>   Without, our shame; within, our consciences;
> Angels and grace, eternall hopes and fears.
>
>   Yet all these fences and their whole aray
>   One cunning bosome-sinne blows quite away.[5]

Herbert knew that he asked, of himself and us, more than could be achieved, but argued, 'it is a good strife to go as farre as wee can in pleasing of him, who hath done so much for us'.[6] In that sense George Herbert is only telling us that the job of a priest is never done and never easy. You will find the same insight elsewhere, memorably in the work of another priest-poet, R. S. Thomas, who refers rather starkly to clergy who 'have a long way to go'.[7] Then, secondly, we need to know that Herbert wrote with a particular style, wrote as a rhetorician. There is an unfamiliar set of assumptions here. Rhetoric is not just about the words you choose, it is concerned with the response you want to evoke. *The Countrey Parson* was never meant to be a textbook on ministry, it is more like a prayer book. As Philip Sheldrake points out, 'The book is meant not simply to *instruct* but to *move* the reader to a deepening sense of call.'[8] This book is an invitation to meditate on the challenge of ministry and contemplate the possibility it might not be an unqualified success. Some contemporary studies of ministry have suggested that the job is difficult and that we might need to be armed or defended. George Herbert thought we might need to reflect on sin and forgiveness.[9]

Like Chrysostom, Herbert believed that ministry had its roots in the commission to Peter, 'feed my sheep'. He thought less about the responsibility of that task, however, and rather more about those who would *receive* this ministry. Herbert was interested in the relationships in ministry. He was not in the least bit sentimental; he knew that priest and people do not naturally make cosy company. Indeed, the real and terrible challenge of living in a parish in relationship becomes evident in the opening words of the first chapter of *The Countrey Parson*: 'A Pastor is the Deputy of Christ for the reducing of Man to the Obedience of God.' The language is slightly opaque if you are not brought up (as Herbert was) with Latin learning. *Duco* means 'to lead' and 're*duc*ing' therefore does not mean 'subjugating', but 'leading back'. It is the language of sin and forgiveness again. Priest and people together are children of the Fall. We are 'welt'ring in sin' and need to find our way home.[10] This is not glamorous work; the enemy is sin and it is petty and grubby.

So Herbert was interested in character. There is a good deal about manner and restraint in *The Countrey Parson*. Priests, Herbert argued, are made not by study but by mastering their emotions and their longings: 'The greatest and hardest preparation is within.' Ordination needs to change you, permanently, and to leave you forever conscious of role and responsibility:

Before they are in Orders, they may be received for Companions, or discoursers; but after a man is once Minister, he cannot agree to come into any house, where he shall not exercise what he is, unless he forsake his plough, and look back.[11]

The Countrey Parson sets a target. Isaak Walton, one of George Herbert's first biographers, tells us that when Herbert was instituted at Bemerton and went into the church to toll the bell, he stayed there some time, prostrate before the altar, and admitted to a friend soon after that 'he set some rules to himself'.[12] For Herbert it was character not task that mattered; ministry requires, above all, a particular kind of life. So, when he came to describe 'the Countrey Parson's Library', the fundamental resource for his teaching and preaching, Herbert did not begin with the books he had read.

> The Countrey Parson's Library is a holy Life: for besides the blessing that that brings upon it, there being a promise, that if the Kingdome of God be first sought, all other things shall be added, even it selfe is a Sermon.[13]

Now, we need to let a little of the cold light of day in among the shades of the sanctuary at this point. George Herbert's commitment to the little broken down church in Bemerton is indeed startling. Admirers of George Herbert talk about his 'conversion'. We must not be blind, though, to the move he made. The parish in Bemerton was on the edge of Wilton Park and Wilton Park was the family home of the Earls of Pembroke, the family home of *his* family. We know that George Herbert was spiritual adviser and friend to the Fourth Earl's wife, Lady Anne Clifford. Bemerton was a very particular place and Herbert's vocation was worked out in a very particular way. To say that is not to suggest that there is anything 'fake' about Herbert's holiness, it is just to point out that it was *his* holiness, worked out in *his* life, and to be reminded that he wrote *The Countrey Parson* as a particular kind of book.

The tone of *The Countrey Parson* is cool, but it is not without realism. It is broken into short chapters: 'The Parson's Knowledge', 'The Parson's Courtesy', 'The Parson's Completeness'. Together they added up to a kind of balance: scripture combined with holiness, mixed in with knowledge about 'pastorage' and 'tillage' and the things that his people would know.[14] For all his idealism he never set out to make life more difficult for those around him, 'because Countrey people live hardly, and therefore as feeling their own sweat, and consequently knowing the price of mony, are offended much with any, who by hard usage increase their travel'.[15]

Over and again, Herbert picked his way between a passionate commitment to holiness (which can make us strange), and the commitment which would make him one with his people. So, there is practical advice. He wrote about preaching (he thought that the pulpit was the parson's 'joy and throne') and knew that his sophisticated rhetorical skills needed to be fitted for the place and for the people. It has to be admitted, at this point, that his patrician background could make him condescending: 'Countrey people; which are thick, and heavy, and hard to raise to a poynt of Zeal, and fervency, and need a mountaine of fire to kindle them; but stories and sayings they will well remember.' He knew that ministry calls us to serve different people differently. He fashioned that insight into one of the best bits of advice on preaching in any manual. He recognized the need to think of the audience not as one, but as many:

> particularizing of his speech now to the younger sort, then to the elder, now to the poor, and now to the rich. This is for you, and This is for you; for particulars ever touch, and awake more then generals.

I used to work with a colleague who imagined, as he wrote a sermon, that some of the members of the congregation sat round his desk (the secretary of the PCC over there, and here a recently confirmed teenager, there an elderly woman faithful for a lifetime). He would look up and reflect on what he was saying to each of them: 'This is for you.'

The services of the Anglican Church in the sixteenth and seventeenth centuries were services of the *word*. The diet of the people of God was psalm, scripture and sermon, and it mattered to Herbert, and to others, how it was served. At Leighton Bromswold, Herbert had the church reordered and twin pulpits built so that preaching and reading the service could enjoy an equal dignity. Prayer was to be delivered attentively:

his voyce is humble, his words treatable, and slow; yet not so slow neither, to let the fervency of the supplicant hang and dy between speaking, but with a grave livelinesse, between fear and zeal, pausing yet pressing, he performes his duty.[16]

Microphones and loudspeakers have changed the way we speak. We do not need to work as hard as we did and we consequently think less about how we speak. It is worth noting that Herbert was not just concerned with audibility; tone was just as important.

'Pausing yet pressing' – it's a glimpse of Herbert's spirituality caught for ever between the hesitancy of the sinner who will always draw back and the eagerness of the lover who will plunge on. It was spirituality 'in ordinary', worked out in the routines of daily life. Admittedly, at times his tone is unfamiliar and uncomfortable. He favoured severity with servants, he demanded a disciplined piety from his children and had a gloomily functional understanding of marriage. If a priest really must marry, his wife should be primarily a partner in ministry.[17] We might want to express it very differently now, but we still need to recognize that it is in leisure, and in the home, that the habits of piety are most easily undone. We know that Herbert was not a dour man; he loved music and was remembered for his quiet charm, but he did not think that ministry would be either easy or amusing. Priests see sin and misery and understand both: 'The Countrey Parson is generally sad, because hee knows nothing but the Crosse of Christ, his minde being defixed on it with those nailes wherewith his Master was.'[18]

The last chapter of *The Countrey Parson* deals with 'Detraction'. It is a study of the problems of dealing with criticism and complaint, the stories you hear, the action you must take. Herbert finds it a difficult subject. Try to silence complaint altogether and you will never discover the places where real evil thrives, but seek it out and you become a gossip. His hostility to sin made him startlingly robust in his commitment to naming and shaming. Yet, reaching that view, he issued a warning against the smug enthusiasm of finding fault with other people.

The Countrey Parson was once recommended in ordination charges to fresh generations of curates. Ronald Blythe describes the book as Herbert's 'rule for English country clergymen'. I know of a priest who read both this book and Baxter each year. Others are not so sure. David Osborne turns on Herbert with elegant fury:

> The Country Parson moves gracefully from seventeenth century Wiltshire to the neverland of English mythology. Maybe now he has a bicycle rather than a horse and carriage, but he is the same man, of a piece with the image that sells loaves of wholemeal bread, shelves of books and racks of calendars, and draws people from towns and cities to holidays or retirement in the English countryside.[19]

The model of ministry worked out in Bemerton, the argument goes, belongs to another age and another place and does not travel well. Not so long ago I bowled down quiet Cotswold roads to a famously picturesque village to preach at a harvest festival. I met the patron of the living, whose ancestors had for several generations been rectors, and discovered that, while he still lived locally, his old family home was now a plush hotel. I sat at supper with another man who clearly cared passionately about the church and its people and was deeply involved in the life of the community. His accent, however, suggested he was not a local man, and it turned out that he was an American banker who had settled in the village in extraordinarily active retirement. Rural England is a complicated place. Leaving them, I fell over in the dark and was reminded, uncomfortably, that I was used to street lights and really was a stranger here.

Try to read *The Countrey Parson* as a textbook and you will find that David Osborne is right; it begins to sound unrealistic. It is not a textbook, it never was a textbook, it is a 'rule'. There can be no textbook, no manual. We do this differently in different places because we are different people. The fascination with task and competence is supposed to make the enormity of vocation manageable, but all it does is add another layer of demand. Worse than that, it deflects us from the one question that matters, 'Can I hold my humanity and my ministry together without compromising either?' Can I be *authentic*? George Herbert's poetry is littered with the evidence of a terrible conflict. He was 'full of rebellion', and 'venom'; he had a 'saplesse' heart, and mere 'shreds of holinesse'. It is a sorry catalogue of 'most foul transgression, wretch crumme of dust a brittle crazy glass'. At its worst it was a treadmill that Herbert worked.[20]

> Sorrie I am, my God, sorrie I am,
> That my offences course it in a ring.[21]

This is what *The Countrey Parson* is really about, a priest's struggle and determination to resist temptation and live in holiness. It is where the book begins and where it ends with his prayers 'Before' and 'After Sermon'. The same radical certainty about the difference between holiness and sin is there:

> How shall we dare to appear before thy face, who are contrary to thee, in all we call thee? for we are darknesse, and weaknesse, and filthinesse, and shame. Misery and sin fill our days: yet art thou our Creatour, and we thy work.[22]

We have begun to set aside *The Countrey Parson*, telling one another that it is outdated and not for us. In itself, that decision does not matter very much; there will always be books we like and books we do not like. The vigorous, angry rejection of George Herbert, however, speaks of a more serious malaise. As ministry becomes more specialist, as we define the tasks in ministry more closely (she thinks of herself as a leader in mission, while he regards himself as a pastor, and I believe I am a teacher), we lose the capacity to talk to one another. We come out of different experiences of training, and we value different parts of our previous experience (and we have more previous experience than we had, because we are ordained later in life). We inhabit different roles as stipendiaries, SSMs, OLMs and House for Duty priests. We are now losing the ability to hold these differences within a common framework.

We do not assume that there is a culture, or a practice, that we share. In fact, very often, we want to stress our differences, ask for *bespoke* training and fashion a distinctive vision. George Herbert gets a good going over not because he is out-dated, but because he has been the presiding voice for so long and we do not trust that voice any more. If we look to practice, or experience, we will always notice that you do things differently from me and I feel things differently from you. Reading *The Countrey Parson*, or any other reflection on ministry, as a handbook we are likely to come away disappointed or even enraged. We need to notice that George Herbert did not set out to be good at his job, he tried to follow Christ.

Heart-work and heaven-work

Facing a mounting sense of crisis, the call to re-evangelize the nation when our resources are more and more constrained, our problem is not that our vision is too big, our problem is that we are getting too specific. We define ministries and tasks when we should tell the bigger, better story about the life of God revealed in Christ, which provides the common language for faith and for ministry. George Herbert tried to make the story of sin and redemption a story about us all, so that we could feel it and share it. It is the truth that Richard Baxter observed about Herbert: '*Herbert* speaks *to God* like one that *really believeth a God*, and whose business in the world is most *with God. Heart-work* and *Heaven-work* make up his Books.'[23] So, when Herbert wrote the poem 'The Priesthood', he wrestled with his anxiety about living up to the calling, being what he must truly be.

> But thou art fire, sacred and hallow'd fire;
> And I but earth and clay: should I presume
> To wear thy habit, the severe attire
> My slender compositions might consume.
> I am both foul and brittle; much unfit
>   To deal in holy Writ.[24]

The Countrey Parson is not an invitation to set up home in a rural Neverland. It is a book about the common language of Christian experience: how to be holy and still belong.

The Church of England is now forced to acknowledge that it can barely sustain its commitment to the parochial structure. Dioceses across the country are experimenting with 'minsters', 'mission communities', 'clusters' and 'hubs'; new structures with new rules of engagement. In this radical enterprise, *The Countrey Parson* has all but disappeared; we do not do that now. We are in danger of missing the point. Energy goes into reimaging the *shape* of ministry. The *content*, however, is the same. It is still all about how you relate to whatever community it is that you find and how you stay true. We need a language we can use that reminds us that the ministry of the Church is a ministry we share. We need that language urgently, before we drift away from one another, shaking our heads more in sorrow than in anger and bemoaning the fact that no one really understands us. We learn from Greenwood and the *Didache* that ministry must not seduce us into putting the clergy centre stage and making ministry into a project. George Herbert's achievement is to set before us the real narrative, the story of sin and salvation, that is the experience and practice of every ministry.

Notes

1 Thomas Aquinas, *Summa Theologica*, II-II.81.8.

2 Quoted in R. Williams, *Silence and Honey Cakes: The Wisdom of the Desert*, Oxford: Lion, 2004, p. 43.

3 On Herbert's saintliness, see, for example, A. Russell, *The Country Parish*, London: SPCK, 1986, pp. 203–5; on the 'myth', see, for example, D. Osborne, *The Country Vicar*, London: Darton, Longman & Todd, 2004, pp. 63–78.

4 G. Herbert, 'The Authour to the Reader', *The Countrey Parson* I, in F. E. Hutchinson (ed.), *The Works of George Herbert*, Oxford: Oxford University Press, 1941. Subsequent Herbert quotes are taken from this edition. There are many editions of *The Countrey Parson*, for example, *The Complete Works in Verse and Prose of George Herbert*, ed. A. B. Grosart (London: 1874; Oxford: Oxford University Press, 1941), which is available online at http://anglicanhistory.org/herbert/parson.html.

5 G. Herbert, 'Sinne (I)', in Hutchinson (ed.), *Works*.

6 Herbert, 'The Authour to the Reader'.

7 R. S. Thomas, 'The Priest', *Collected Poems*, London: Orion, 1979, p. 196.

8 P. Sheldrake, *Heaven in Ordinary: George Herbert and his Writings*, London: Canterbury Press, 2009, p. 11.

9 See, for example, A. Clitherow, *Renewing Faith in Ordained Ministry: New Hope for Tired Clergy*, London: SPCK, 2004; M. Dudley and V. Rounding, *The Parish Survival Guide*, London: SPCK, 2004.

10 G. Herbert, 'The Glance', in Hutchinson (ed.), *Works*.

11 Herbert, *The Countrey Parson*, II.

12 I. Walton, *The Life of Mr. George Herbert* (1675), para. 45.

13 Herbert, *The Countrey Parson*, XXXIII.

14 Herbert, *The Countrey Parson*, IIII.

15 Herbert, *The Countrey Parson*, III.

16 Herbert, *The Countrey Parson*, VI.

17 Herbert, *The Countrey Parson*, IX.

18 Herbert, *The Countrey Parson*, XXVII.

19 Osborne, *The Country Vicar*, p. 69, and see M. Grundy, *What they Don't Teach you at Theological College*, Norwich: Canterbury Press, 2003, p. 10, and J. Lewis-Anthony, *If You Meet George Herbert on the Road, Kill Him: Radically Re-Thinking Priestly Ministry*, London: Mowbray, 2009.

20 I owe this insight to Helen Vendler.

21 G. Herbert, 'Sinnes Round', in Hutchinson (ed.), *Works*.

22 Herbert, 'The Author's Prayer Before Sermon', *The Countrey Parson*.

23 Quoted in C. Malcolmson, *Heart-Work: George Herbert and the Protestant Ethic*, Stanford, CA: Stanford University Press, 1999, p. 1, and see how she develops the argument (p. 138).

24 'The Priesthood', lines 7–12, from *The Temple*, in Hutchinson (ed.), *Works*.

7

Holiness

The chariots of Israel

'Always a henchman' – that is how Francis Paget, the Bishop
of Oxford, dismissed the life and work of Henry Parry Liddon.
'Always a henchman', in short, never quite his own man. The
Dictionary of National Biography is kinder, but makes exactly
the same point, describing Liddon as a man who could not
throw off the mantle of 'the disciple'. Liddon lived in the shade
of the heroes of his youth: Keble and Pusey. His ministry was
at the service of theirs. Keble died in 1866, but Pusey lived on
until 1882, a bent and brooding presence in Christ Church,
where Liddon also kept rooms. His hand was over Liddon,
nudging the course of his Bampton Lectures and inhibiting him
from making any memorial to Darwin. Paget was too brutal,
however; it was not weakness that constrained Liddon, it was
loyalty and affection. He was not completely wrong – loyalty
and affection have a place in ministry.

Ordained ministry, like all Christian discipleship, is the
answer to a call. It is a work in progress and it is not a contract.
The clergy of the Church of England have role descriptions,
priorities and quite possibly a mission action plan. Some of
them have work consultants and lots of them have strategies.
They have staff meetings, they carry diaries. These men and
women plan what they will do and then they examine how
well they are doing it in development reviews. Even so, the
really significant question at ordination is not about what you
are going to *do*; it is altogether much more interesting to ask
what you will *become*. Ordination, like every other Christian
vocation, is just a direction of travel. Of course, there is a very

demanding job of work to do. So the clergy have to step into an office set about with expectations, and they must meet at least some of those expectations. We expect them to be focused and busy, but we also require them to live in Christ. We look for character at least as much as we look for action. They must work, live in Christ and be themselves. Ordination must never be a performance. Ministry has always been set about with temptations to use the role as a platform or shield. Chaucer, Jane Austen, Anthony Trollope and others nailed that temptation years ago. All that has to be resisted, but, because ordination is a call, it will change a person. In ministry you must never pretend to be what you are not and still accept that Christ calls you to be more than you are. Ministry will change you. Liddon, who spent years reflecting on priesthood, went back to Cuddesdon, the college where he had taught, to preach at an anniversary in 1873. He took it as read that there was a power at work within a college that would transform the students.

> It pours itself around others, when and how they know not; it saturates them; it impregnates them with its own fervour and impetuosity; it insensibly furnishes them with new points of view, new moods of feeling, new estimates of life; they learn, like the converted Franks, to adore what they had burned, and to burn what they had adored, before they know it.[1]

At the ordination service the clergy are charged to grow into the likeness of Christ and promise to fashion their lives and their households 'according to the way of Christ'. They declare that they will be changed and they wonder what the change will be. Small wonder, then, that they look for clues about what they might become in the lives of the clergy they know. Someone else's ministry can be a stimulus and a spur to an ordinand. When I first thought about my own vocation I latched on to the work and personality of a curate in the parish where I grew up. He provided the link between an idea about ordination and the life of a priest. He provided some definition and shape for what I thought about ministry, though he did not know that was what he was doing. I began my own ministry relying on loyalty and affection. The problem is that, in time, the definition you borrow can become a burden. Try asking a group of curates about a ministry that has influenced them (I have); they will come up with plenty of examples. Try asking the same questions to more seasoned incumbents (I have); you will find they have become more cautious. A priest may spend a few months acquiring a bit of inherited behaviour and then decades struggling out of what was always a borrowed skin. It took me three years and more to stop preaching sermons that were a poor pastiche of what I had heard from the man who was Vice-Principal of Cuddesdon when I trained there. At best this is a harmless bit of growing up, at worst it is a struggle with a false identity. Ironically, Liddon, who so struggled with the influence of his own idols, was himself an idol to others. Samuel Wilberforce, the Bishop of Oxford, who lived next to the college in Cuddesdon when Liddon worked there, admired Liddon's ministry, but grumbled that the students were picking up his mannerisms. He thought the culture of the college was affected. Ministry has always been modelled for us. Liddon was far from unusual in feeling Pusey's influence. His problem perhaps was that the lessons he learnt were so hard to shake off because Liddon learned from giants.

He is not well known now. He had a brief, if brilliant, career training clergy at Cuddesdon, but preaching was his great gift and his life's work. After he was made canon of St Paul's, services had to be moved into the nave in order to accommodate the crowds that came. But fame as a preacher is always time limited. Pusey (inevitably) had something to say about that: 'You preach sermons an hour long at St. Paul's, and nobody hears you, and you are knocked up a fortnight afterwards. You have done nothing.'[2] Read the sermons now and you can marvel at the prose and the passion, but you cannot help observing that this ministry would not be possible now. Liddon belonged to a literary culture that once shaped the English church and the English clergy. We did things differently then. Lancelot Andrewes gave over his morning to study in the late sixteenth century and, in the 1950s, R. S. Thomas was still doing the same (while spending at least some of his afternoons walking and birdwatching).[3] These are not practices that have found their way into modern documents about the role and responsibility of the clergy. So let's be clear: if we read Liddon now (or, indeed, most of the other authors named here), we are confronted with a vision of ministry that is fashioned for different times. Practice and assumptions have changed; these individuals, these ministries, can feel alien and even irrelevant.

So, why should we bother with these long dead priests and opinions wrestled from such different experience? We have to bother because ministry belongs to them as much as it belongs to us. Ministry is something we inherit, inhabit and then bequeath. Ministry is a succession, a conversation over time, by turns building on foundations others lay and starting something new. Elisha prayed for a double portion of the spirit of Elijah and, when Elijah ascended into the heavens, burst out, 'Father, father! The chariots of Israel and its horsemen.'[4] Melanchthon chose that same text to announce the death of his master Luther in Wittenberg. If it is a mistake to turn ministry into performance, it is another equally serious mistake to turn it into a possession, as though it is just ours and depends on us. If we get stuck trying too hard to be someone else (trying to preach like the Vice-Principal) we are in trouble. If we get stuck thinking we have arrived, that we have ministry sorted and defined, we are equally in danger. In both cases ministry has become a possession. It is either what someone else had that we want, or it is something we think we own and will now never let go. Ministry is not a possession, it is a gift. All these books on ministry cited here, and all this opinion, are not intended to tell us how to do this. We will each of us work that out for ourselves. They are here to remind us that the business of working it out for ourselves never stops; here to remind us that ministry is shared, inherited, bequeathed, and always a work in progress. We become bad historians when we venerate the past and make, for example, the Oxford Movement into a golden age. We are also bad historians when we think the past is a curse we have to shake off and convince ourselves that we face a modern crisis that only we can negotiate. Our problem is not that we want to make ministry new, it must be constantly refreshed. Our problem is our growing conviction that we have the *only* answer. There is a new sense of urgency in the Church that is welcome, but there can be an impatience that comes with urgency and a narrowing of focus that is less welcome.

Henry Parry Liddon

Liddon knew about ministry that was new and yet informed. Forced by ill health to abandon his own parochial ministry, he was Vice Principal of the new theological college at Cuddesdon from 1854 until 1859. Prior to the creation of places like Cuddesdon, men (and they were, of course, all men) who presented themselves to a bishop for ordination were examined, with more or less diligence, and were then ordained, perhaps after a short period of preparation, quite possibly in the episcopal dining room. It was an elegant, gentlemanly and rather curious arrangement. A letter written by a young priest in 1841, 13 years before Cuddesdon was opened, gives us a glimpse of that extraordinary, lost world:

> The Ordination was conducted in the most comfortable manner ... Arrayed in full canonicals, the flowing sleeves of his surplice floating on the breeze which his flight from the drawing-room to the Chapel occasioned, [the Bishop's Chaplain] smilingly handed a galaxy of beauty and fashion to their cushioned seats. When all men were seated in breathless expectation the sleeves were heard in the distance, and presently appeared the Chaplain, leading in the Bishopess, the first of a long procession of children and maidservants; all the candidates, except myself and one or two others, arose, and testified their respect. Lastly the Bishop entered (all men on the tip-toe of expectation) wearing the Order of the Garter.[5]

Cuddesdon was created in a determined bid to free ministry from the drawing room. Samuel Wilberforce, Bishop of Oxford and founder of the college, explained his vision of what was needed, in a conversation with Alfred Pott, the first Principal:

The want of clerical tone, and of religious habits, which the Bishop noted in some of his intercourse with some of the younger clergy, had a great deal to do with his proposals. Residence in such a college as he contemplated would, in his judgement, do much to foster such a tone and habit as he desired to see.[6]

He may have called it 'tone and habit', but Wilberforce wanted to see what we would now call 'formation'. He believed that priesthood was not a set of functions, but a character, and a character that could be learnt. Liddon agreed with him. A term into his time in Cuddesdon, he identified what he thought to be the hallmark of what a college should be:

A habituation to religious practice and thoughts – in short spiritual training. We have accordingly endeavoured to lay great emphasis on this part of our system; without neglecting the intellectual side of churchmanship.[7]

In the pages of the *Didache* we have recognized that the community has needs that must be met. We have seen in Ignatius that there is a language that must be learnt, and in Carr that there is a context and a task to acknowledge. Liddon would not have dissented from any of those insights, but he was most interested in the personality and character that would sustain this burden. At Cuddesdon he threw himself into the task with a will and he proved so effective in creating 'tone' that the bishop was soon complaining it had all got far too peculiar.[8]

In two sermons, preached after he had left Cuddesdon, Liddon worked out his ideas about theological training in a more systematic way. The stress was always the same; the stress was always on holiness. He believed, passionately, that ordinands needed to learn theology. It was not that he wanted them to be clever; he wanted them to have hope. Liddon argued that theology feeds the imagination; a theologically informed mind can break out of the straitjacket of expectation and imagine what redemption might be like; it can picture heaven. Without theological resources the clergy can only offer their own experience to set against the experiences they encounter. Liddon could be sharp, a parish will not

> be satisfied with sentiments when it craves for truths. The conception of an untheological religion is one of those desperate shifts to which men are driven when they have lost all vital, intellectual hold upon the bone and substance of the Faith.[9]

So theology mattered. Even so, character always mattered more. Liddon did not want colleges that might teach students, he wanted colleges that would change them. It was a task that no university could tackle, a work of both soul *and* intellect. Liddon argued that the job of the college was to confront its students with some basic questions: 'What does he mean by taking orders? Why does he choose this rather than any other walk in life? ... Is he intending to follow a respectable profession, or has he, in his secret soul, given himself to God?'[10] Here we get to the heart of the staggering moral and intellectual seriousness that characterizes so much nineteenth-century writing on ministry.

> Many a man enters here, with good dispositions, with a purpose to serve God in the Sacred Ministry, entertained, it may be, since childhood, yet with all that light-heartedness of temper and that hazy perception of the stern lines of truth which are natural at twenty-two. [St. John xxi. 18.] He is in the position of the sons of Zebedee; he wishes to sit on the right hand or on the left; he knows not what he asks. [St. Mark x. 37.] It is then the duty of a college like this to unveil to him the cup of which Christ once drank, and the baptism with which Christ was baptized, gently, considerately, yet sincerely.[11]

It sounds high-minded and it was. Liddon knew that, even then, this was unfamiliar and unwelcome language. 'The feeling is, that you would just as soon refer to a man's income, or to the character of his near relations, as to his daily prayers.'[12]

Liddon wrote about holiness; he wanted the clergy to be trained in holiness. That idea was hardly new, but Liddon was one of the first to suggest that ordinands could be set apart to train for this. He was scathing about the generations that had passed too easily from university into the Church's ministry, 'a continuous stream of life and energy – from the lectures, the boats, the unions, the college chapels, the haunts and associations which are often too degrading to bear mention, – to the pulpits, the deathbeds, the altars of the Church of Jesus Christ'.[13] Liddon thought that the clergy had become suspicious of anything that might mark them out: 'they neglect to do anything with their souls or bodies'.[14] He was determined to teach ordinands an 'inner life', tell them how to inhabit the emotions and ideas they would call on in places of pain and despair. He wanted them to speak with conviction of truths they had learnt to rely on themselves. He quoted John James Blunt, the Lady Margaret Professor of Divinity in Cambridge:

> After all is said and done the parish priest can never be thoroughly effective in the sick-room till his own heart shall be in a condition to furnish him readily with the language he should employ in it. He cannot work conviction in another ... of the unspeakable comfort contained in the doctrines of the Cross, till in his own very self he has tasted what that comfort is ... this is not a lesson to be learned from a professor in the schools, but is to be gathered by self-discipline and self restraint, in the silence of night, and the chamber amidst the disappointments, the disasters, the vanities, the distresses of life.[15]

It is easy to mistake the point that Liddon was making. Surrounded by tragedy, we have learnt, rather late in the day, that we need to let the victims of tragedy tell their stories. We listen more than we did, and high time too. Our difficulty is that we are less sure of our theology than we were. We study theology less, we make it less of a priority and, as a consequence, as we listen more, we also say less. There is not much of what Liddon called 'the bone and substance of our faith'. That quotation from Blunt could be read as an invitation to believe that ministry is just the sharing of experience – when

I meet your bereavement, I speak of mine. That, though, is an assumption that would drive every ministry into a ghetto: the depressed ministering to the depressed, the bereaved talking to the bereaved, and bishops talking to themselves. Liddon would have dismissed that idea in an instant. Suspicious of 'sentiment', he believed that the clergy learnt the vocabulary they need from reading and from prayer. Ministry doesn't offer sympathy and fellow feeling; it gathers us together in the presence of Christ. Ministry doesn't shut a door to create a special intimacy; it draws back the curtains and throws wide the doors to confront us with the table-turning power of God's justice and love. Insisting on unfashionable words like 'duty' and 'responsibility', Liddon argued that, if we make an effort, we can acquire habits of reflection and understanding that equip us to talk to the strangers in our midst.

Here an idea that was present in Keble gathers pace and force. In both men there was a growing determination to name and catalogue priestly virtues and priestly actions. The aim, of course, was to set a standard and create an expectation, and the standard and expectation was holiness. The difficulty and the danger was that Liddon might ask too much. Here, by way of example, is Liddon discussing the benefits of meditation and being characteristically brutal with anything less than method and real discipline.

> You see a worthy clergyman in his study, – he is resting his elbow on the table, and reflecting on some portion of his Bible – making remarks at intervals to his wife. This is indeed better than nothing, although it be a feeble and dreamy effort, failing in reverence, in intellectual address, in analysis, in stimulating the imagination, in challenging and coercing the will, in opening the soul in very truth to the eye of its God and making it court his gaze ... meditation to be real MUST BE systematic.[16]

The man who wrote this succumbed to the effects of exhaustion in his very early sixties. Holiness is, and always will be, demanding, but perhaps Liddon failed to make the necessary distinction between denying oneself and denying *life* itself. A ministry that models overwork is, ultimately, not a ministry that really celebrates the fullness of life in Christ. Books on ministry either have to mix some water with the wine, or tell us how we can live with our failures. When they do not do that they create a benchmark of sanctity that is out of reach for most of us.

The sermons, though, are wide-ranging. Liddon knew the temptations of ministry from within, 'the love of prominence, the love of influence, the love of popularity and of the praise of men'.[17] For all the rigour with which he directs us to the Book of Common Prayer, study, scripture and meditation, he knew too that the clergy need to be self-aware. Inevitably, a man for whom preaching was such a fundamentally important and demanding task had things to say about preaching. He could be pugnacious in the pulpit and he urged others to preach with the same courage. Preaching must have the nerve to speak the truth.

> There are petty oppositions, petty persecutions, indirect yet powerful influences, which will stay a man's hand, and silence his tongue, even in this age and land of civil freedom; unless his conscience be quick and his will strong, through a constant sight of One Who is the Lord and the Subject of that Truth which He proclaims. He will abridge, soften down, mutilate his message.[18]

All this in a sermon preached at an ordination in Salisbury in 1864. There he urged on those being ordained 'the whole counsel of God'. Liddon felt in himself and saw in others a temptation to confine the gospel and to restrict preaching to something too particular. Preaching must be more than a literary effort; it should have its roots in a preacher wrestling personally with sin and grace and standing in the presence of God. A preacher who settles for less will fail:

> His thought will drift naturally away from the central and most solemn truths to the literary embellishments which

surround the faith; he will toy with questions of geography, or history, or custom, or scene, or dress; he will reproduce with vivid power the personages and events of long-past ages, it may be with the talent of a master-artist; he will give to the human side of Religion the best of his time and of his toil. In doing this he may, after the world's measure, be doing good work; but let us not deceive ourselves – he will not be saving souls.[19]

Urging the clergy to remember their own stake in the story of salvation, and that they spoke as 'a redeemed sinner speaking to redeemed sinners', Liddon sounds like Keble. There is always a temptation to tell people what we have just read, what appeals to us, what might amuse or inform. The trouble is that it is less than the truth. The heart of preaching is the cross, and salvation; all the rest is commentary.

Ten years after the sermon at Salisbury, he preached at an ordination service in St Paul's, where he was a canon. It was a sermon on a text taken from the tenth chapter of St John's Gospel, in which the followers of the murdered John the Baptist encounter Jesus. Meeting at last the man John had described to them, they said, 'John did no miracle: but all things that John spake of this man were true.' Liddon reminded the congregation that John the Baptist, a remarkable man living in remarkable times, 'did no miracle'. Then he turned his attention to those who were to be ordained. He asked them a rather Victorian question: 'What shall I desire to have been, to have done, when I come to die?'[20] He gave those ordinands a list of things to which they might look forward: change of work, the making and losing of friends, great sorrows, great joys, marriage perhaps, promotion even, and told them that none of it mattered. They should have one ambition, he said; they should hope that when their ministry was over men and women would say of them what once they said of John the Baptist, 'John did no miracle: but all things that John spake of this man were true.'

Liddon understood preaching and ministry itself as the steady task of being focused on the life of Christ. It would be enough 'if quietly, perseveringly, unflinchingly, we have kept our eye on Him'.[21] The temptation to look at something else, talk about something else, is often almost overwhelming. The temptation to spend your time watching yourself in this extraordinary role is indeed also overwhelming. At the ordination in St Paul's in 1874, and in ordinations before and since, the scriptures are handed to the candidates for ordination:

> *Then the Bishop shall deliver to every one of them kneeling the Bible into his hand, saying,*
> Take thou Authority to preach the Word of God, and to minister the holy Sacraments in the Congregation, where thou shalt be lawfully appointed thereunto.[22]

In 1439, when people worried about exactly where and when the decisive moment of ordination came, the Council of Florence ruled that it was this, the giving and receiving of the New Testament, that defined ordination to the diaconate. It is a reminder that the task of the ordained ministry is not to speak about itself, but about Christ. Or, as Liddon put it, 'quietly, perseveringly, unflinchingly, we have kept our eye on Him'. The vocation of all Christ's disciples is to be Christ-like. Authentic vocation is worked out in being more like him and less like ourselves. That is why, Liddon observed, that we all 'look in the lives of the preachers of the Crucified for something that shall stand for the mark of the Nails'.[23] We have a right to expect that.

Gregory of Nazianzus: awestruck

Fashions in ministry change, and Liddon's picture got banished from the ground floor of the college at Cuddesdon just after I left. That was not a judgement on his opinions; I doubt if the committee that got rid of him had read any of his sermons. Liddon's problem was that he was male, and it was too uncomfortable that all the pictures in the main corridor were male. If your history determines all the images you use, you have made your history an idol. If you have stopped reading your history you are just ill informed. Liddon had something important to say and he was not alone in saying it. Holiness, the practice of public holiness, has always been a crucial element in ministry.

Round about Christmas, in the year 361, a father ordained his son, Gregory, in a small town in the mountain country of central Anatolia, a region that was in those days called Cappadocia.[24] A new presbyter was welcome; this was a mission field (the joke then was that a Cappadocian was about as likely to talk good sense as a tortoise was to fly).[25] It was a ministry everyone was going to remember, but it started about as badly as it is possible to start. Gregory promptly fled from Nazianzus, from his father and from priesthood. He hid in the misty hills until Easter, before returning crestfallen: 'I have been defeated, and own my defeat.'[26] Later, he offered a kind of explanation, *The Oration in Defence of his Flight to Pontus.*

Why did he run away? There are a number of different answers to that question. Put simply, he was frightened and resentful. Gregory had not sought ordination out; he had other plans, it was done against his will and he later described it as an act of 'tyranny'. He was, quite simply, overwhelmed by the determination of his father and the local church.[27] While others believed in this vocation of his, he was not sure that he did. Gregory was a scholar; he had sought out learning in Palestinian Caesarea, Alexandria and Athens. He lived in his head and, confronted by the demands of church office, he suddenly knew how much he would miss his books: 'there came over me an eager longing for the blessings of calm and retirement'.[28]

The real crisis for Gregory, however, had nothing to do with the fear of what he didn't know; his problem was rooted in what he *did* know. Gregory had thought about ministry and he thought it was terrifying. It was a challenge that should fill anyone with dread. Like Liddon, he had no time for anyone over-eager for this work:

> I was ashamed of all those others, who, without being better than ordinary people ... intrude into the most sacred offices and before becoming worthy to approach the temples, they

lay claim to the sanctuary, and they push and thrust around the holy table, as if they thought this order to be a means of livelihood, instead of a pattern of virtue.[29]

Little by little, through the work of people like Clement, Irenaeus and Cyprian, the Church had defined what it wanted from its clergy. In Gregory we see the impact that makes. Here was a man who knew what was now asked and feared it.

He was in good company. When the Bible talks about vocation it describes something shattering and overwhelming. Moses heard his own vocation described to him at Horeb. He was fearful and 'hid his face'. As God spelt out the task, Moses argued. He doubted that he had the presence and authority he needed: 'But suppose they do not believe me or listen to me ...' He doubted that he had the ability, 'O my Lord, I have never been eloquent.' When all those strategies of evasion failed, he resorted to the old argument that someone else could do it better: 'O my Lord, please send someone else.' He was only silenced when 'the anger of the LORD was kindled' against him.[30] Similarly, when Isaiah was given a vision of God in the Temple, his first reaction was dismay. His horror is standard fare at ordination services: 'Woe is me! I am lost, for I am a man of unclean lips, and I live among a people of unclean lips.'[31] Even St Peter, impetuous and passionate, famously fell down before Christ and begged, 'Go away from me, Lord, for I am a sinful man!'[32]

That is not the language we use to describe vocation now. Our careful and attentive selection processes are deeply impressive, but they do slightly imply that if you can muster the competencies and reflect appropriately on the right sort of experiences you must be fitted for ministry. Just occasionally we talk as though our task is to advance by inches (and all of them carefully recorded in a learning journal) from *here* to *there*. It is a process that gives us some confidence and keeps us on task, but something has been lost. Christ's ministry began with an extraordinary declaration that the future was breaking out. In that future the blind will be given sight, the lame will walk and a new community will be created in which rich and poor sit at table together under a government of love. If that is the hope then we really cannot map out a journey that will take us, by carefully recorded stages, from a Bishop's Advisory Panel to *there*. Failing to see the full scale of what lies ahead, we can (if we are not careful) end up filling in forms that defend the person that we are from the demands of the person we are called to be.

Gregory of Nazianzus knew the enormity of the challenge in Christian vocation. He knew that he would have to set an example, and that horrified him. More specifically, he knew he must set a *good* example and that goodness often struggles to recommend itself, while sin draws people after it. Suppose he modelled evils for others to follow?

> [G]oodness can with difficulty gain a hold upon human nature, like fire upon green wood; while most men are ready and disposed to join in evil, like stubble, I mean, ready for a spark and a wind, which is easily kindled and consumed from its dryness.[33]

The task was not to *describe* virtue, but to *demonstrate* it. Priests must not become poor models sitting for bad painters.[34] Working on human habits and human passions, working on our own habits and those of a congregation, the craft of the ordained ministry is to change lives.

> [T]he scope of our art is to provide the soul with wings, to rescue it from the world and give it to God, and to watch over that which is in His image, if it abides, to take it by the hand, if it is in danger, or restore it, if ruined, to make Christ to dwell in the heart by the Spirit: and, in short, to deify, and bestow heavenly bliss upon, one who belongs to the heavenly host.[35]

Gregory wanted nothing less than to lift men and women to heaven.

Gregory knew what made him run away. More complex motives took him home. In scripture, he read about Jonah and learnt about obedience; that was significant. But, equally significant was the fact that he missed the community in which he had grown up and missed his parents. Love and duty helped bring him back. Yet he knew his home would now be a different place and have a different feel. He would be set apart. That was an idea that soon became kind of commonplace. Richard Hooker was keenly conscious that ordination creates distance, 'it severeth them that have it from other men'. He knew too that it was demanding: 'the burden thereof is heavy and the charge great'.[36] George Herbert was even more alarmed and alarming in what he had to say about priesthood:

> ... thou art fire, sacred and hallow'd fire;
> And I but earth and clay: should I presume
> To wear thy habit, the severe attire
> My slender compositions might consume.
> I am both foul and brittle; much unfit
> To deal in holy Writ.[37]

No surprise then that, for a contemporary writer like Kenneth Mason, the challenge of priesthood can feel overwhelming and isolating.[38] In an extraordinary parable at the beginning of his book, he compares a priest to the stalker in the Russian film of that name:

> The life has a dangerous, disturbed quality, which could only be sustained by some inner compulsion. The stalker's family relations are strained, his wife wonders what she has married, and the children are famous for their oddity. In society people react strangely to him – admiration, fear, distaste, mingled together.[39]

Admiration and distaste mingled together. We play the vocation down and demean it. We talk the vocation up and then fail. Over and again those of us who are ordained have let the ideal down and rightly suffered exposure for hypocrisy. As Gregory pointed out, our crime is not just to fall into sin, but to make our sin a trap for others. It is a terrible thing to do.

Gregory went home to ministry in Nazianzus acknowledging that Christian faith is never solitary. We live and proclaim the gospel of love, by loving others and being loved. The distinctive characteristic of ordained ministry is that it happens in a community; it is a *public* ministry. In Gregory's words, ministry is committed to 'the perfecting of the church'.[40] He came back for the sake of the Church and out of obedience to God. He did not believe he would accomplish great things. He remained anxious that he might do things he would be ashamed of, but he would have been more ashamed not to try.

Serious about community, Gregory was also serious about sin. His understanding of sin was sophisticated and thoughtful. We trivialize temptation by assuming that there are some straightforward distinctions to be made between good and bad things. Doing that, we assume that we are at risk from the world around us, from bad things that are out there waiting to trip us up. Gregory knew that we are usually tempted by *good* things and struggle with natural desires. So, in a little glimpse of fourth-century psychology, he suggested, 'our warfare is directed against that adversary and foe within us, who uses ourselves as his weapons against ourselves'.[41] He recognized that we are most at risk not from things that we think are somehow 'out there', but from our own instincts and assumptions. That means that, if we are to become the people we should be, we might have to give up on some things that we think are actually characteristic of us. Gregory described that process as 'healing' and thought of the clergy as physicians of the soul. (Gregory's brother was a physician and it seems as if Gregory enjoyed comparing and contrasting their different experience.) It was, for him, the very heart of the gospel, turning from sin is turning from the tree in Eden to the wood of the cross: 'This is the reason for the generation and the virgin, for the manger and Bethlehem ... Bethlehem because of Eden, the manger because of the garden, small and visible things on behalf of great and hidden things.'[42] He argued that the work of the pastor is to find different remedies for different diseases of the soul. Holiness really does not feel natural at first. Commending it, ministers will have to be sophisticated and alert. No general invitation will work; personal holiness will always need to be personally encouraged. There are times to be quiet and times to speak; times to praise and times to blame. Gregory was acutely conscious that his audience contained all sorts and conditions, 'needing like an instrument of many strings, to be played upon in various ways'.[43] Delicate work, and work that the clergy must begin in themselves: 'A man must himself be cleansed, before cleansing others: himself become wise, that he may make others wise; become light, and then give light.'[44]

Gregory did not begin this ministry confident that he had the resources for the challenge ahead. 'I did not, nor do I now, think myself qualified to rule a flock or herd, or to have authority over the souls of men.'[45] He ran away because he knew the task was beyond him. He returned because he could not escape it. His vocation was a lifelong encounter with a voice that could not be ignored; it was simply the summons to work out his salvation in the way that had been put before him.

John Chrysostom: walking with angels

Just 20 years after Gregory's ordination another, apparently reluctant, candidate wrestled with vocation. John, born *c.* 349, would later be Archbishop in Constantinople and named 'Chrysostom' (golden-mouthed). He had a talent for controversy, and controversy attended him. Just how it all began is a bit of a puzzle. Chrysostom later claimed that when he was in his mid-twenties he got wind of a plot to ordain both him and a close friend, Basil, as bishops and that he conspired to ensure Basil was ordained while he went into hiding.[46] That at least is the story he tells in the treatise he wrote, *On the Priesthood*.[47] It is a good story and some accept it at face value, pursing their lips with disapproval: 'John Chrysostom considered priesthood the highest calling, but avoided ordination by deceit.'[48] Others wonder if the story behind Chrysostom's treatise is really a rhetorical device and are a touch suspicious that so soon after Gregory's extraordinary *Oration in Defence of Flight* Chrysostom appeared to muscle in on a successful franchise.[49]

On the Priesthood is presented in the form of a (slightly stilted) dialogue between Basil and Chrysostom. It is written with theological purpose, not as personal testimony. Chrysostom wants to show that ordination has its origin in a direct command given by Christ. Years earlier, Clement had suggested that Christ called apostles, and apostles then commissioned bishops and deacons, thus demonstrating (at least to his own satisfaction) that one ministry derived from another.[50] Chrysostom was more ambitious and offered up a rather supple reading of the conversation between Christ and Peter at the lakeside. Generally, we assume that when Christ asked Peter 'Do you love me?' it was a real question. Peter had denied Christ three times and there were good grounds for Christ to question his commitment three times. Chrysostom, however, suggested that Christ was sure of Peter's love and was much more interested in the obligations of ministry. What Christ was doing was instructing Peter that those who *do* love him are called to a particular task; they are to 'feed his sheep'.

> He might have said to him, 'If thou lovest me practise fasting, sleeping on the ground, and prolonged vigils, defend the wronged, be as a father to orphans, and supply the place of a husband to their mother.' But as a matter of fact, setting aside all these things, what does He say? 'Tend my sheep.'[51]

So, Chrysostom shifted the focus of ministry. Where once (in the *Didache*, for example) the emphasis had fallen on the fact that Christ called apostles to mission, now Chrysostom asks us to acknowledge that what Christ instituted was a ministry of oversight, 'tending the sheep'. The *Didache* would make us ambassadors, but Chrysostom would have us govern. Chrysostom also pointed out that Christ asked Peter, 'Do you love me more than these?' and argued that Peter's calling was superior to the task committed to the rest of the apostles. Peter was commissioned to 'preside over the church' and to take responsibility for 'the care of so many souls'. It was a staggeringly demanding task. Chrysostom was clear it was a burden few can bear:

[W]e must bring forward those who to a large extent surpass all others and soar as much above them in excellence of spirit as Saul overtopped the whole Hebrew nation in bodily stature … let the distinction between the pastor and his charge be as great as that between rational man and irrational creatures.[52]

Chrysostom did not try to define ministry by making comparisons. He never suggested that ministry is a bit like being a conductor, or a teacher. The point about ordained ministry was that it was precisely *unlike* anything else. To be in ministry is to engage in spiritual warfare. He quoted the Epistle to the Ephesians: 'We wrestle not against flesh and blood, but against principalities, against powers, against the rulers of the darkness of this world, against spiritual wickedness in high places.'[53] Then, Chrysostom rehearsed arguments that would have been familiar to Gregory of Nazianzus. The particular challenge of the ministry is that a poor minister might damage Christ's precious flock. While Gregory thought the clergy give wings to a soul and 'rescue it from the world', Chrysostom's vision was even more striking (and alarming). He believed that priests walked with angels:

For the priestly office is indeed discharged on earth, but it ranks amongst heavenly ordinances; and very naturally so: for neither man, nor angel, nor archangel, nor any other created power, but the Paraclete Himself, instituted this vocation, and persuaded men while still abiding in the flesh to represent the ministry of angels. Wherefore the consecrated priest ought to be as pure as if he were standing in the heavens themselves in the midst of those powers.[54]

Chrysostom was motivated in part by a liturgical interest that did not surface in Gregory. He thought about priests standing at the altar where they must administer 'things which are in Heaven'.[55] The effect, of such an exalted theology of priesthood was precisely the effect that Gregory had observed and dreaded. Priests who fail to live up to the calling can do terrible damage:

For the faults of ordinary men, being committed as it were in the dark, ruin only those who practise them: but the errors of a man in a conspicuous position, and known to many, inflicts a common injury upon all.[56]

Priests can do terrible things to other people and priests can do terrible things to themselves. In an extraordinary passage, Chrysostom set out the peculiar temptations and trials that priesthood brings:

[I]f any one were to commit this charge to me, it would be all the same as if he tied my hands behind my back, and delivered me to the wild beasts dwelling on that rock to rend me in pieces day by day. Do you ask what those wild beasts are? They are wrath, despondency, envy, strife, slanders, accusations, falsehood, hypocrisy, intrigues, anger against those who have done no harm, pleasure at the indecorous acts of fellow ministers, sorrow at their prosperity, love of praise, desire of honour (which indeed most of all drives the human soul headlong to perdition), doctrines devised to please, servile flatteries, ignoble fawning, contempt of the poor, paying court to the rich, senseless and mischievous honours, favours attended with danger both to those who offer and those who accept them, sordid fear suited only to the basest of slaves, the abolition of plain speaking, a great affectation of humility, but banishment of truth, the suppression of convictions and reproofs, or rather the excessive use of them against the poor, while against those who are invested with power no one dare open his lips.[57]

It is not an exhaustive list. Chrysostom appears to have been less threatened by the temptations of intimacy than some. He had an eye for two significant challenges. The clergy talk, they preach and teach, they give advice. People listen to what they have to say. Chrysostom, trained in the great schools of rhetoric, knew the temptations of speech. In simple terms, it is the danger that you will say too little or too much. A priest can smother the truth in platitudes and call it pastoral care. A priest can say brave words to those who will not answer back, but be mealy-mouthed with those who can.

That is one challenge. The other danger that Chrysostom identified is that the clergy become much too aware of one another. In that famous scene at the lakeside, which was so decisive for Chrysostom's own theology of ministry, Peter was reconciled with Christ. At that critical moment, forgiven the past and commissioned for the future, Peter looks up and wants to know about someone else: 'Peter turned and saw the disciple whom Jesus loved following them ... When Peter saw him, he said to Jesus, "Lord, what about him?"'[58] It has been one of the besetting sins of clergy ever since, to lose focus on what Christ asks of us because we are more interested in what might be expected of someone else. It is our own salvation that we must live out; we cannot have our eyes on following Christ when we are looking at someone else.

Reading Chrysostom is a challenge. It can be hard to follow where he wants to lead. A theology that suggests that a priest is called to be human and forgiven seems to have more to commend it than a theology that thinks a priest must be heroic and appalled. Even so, both Chrysostom and Gregory remind us of something significant. Christian vocation is serious and full of possibility. It confronts us with the scale and size of the hope that is set before us. We should be awestruck, like Emily Dickinson, by the possibilities.

> The only news I know
> Is bulletins all day
> From immortality.[59]

What Gregory and Chrysostom spotted is that the clergy have to work out these possibilities in public, with all the attendant dangers that they will disgrace themselves and drag others down with them.

Richard Baxter: a great and serious business

In 2011 the St Pius X Press reissued a book by the Dominican scholar Reginald Garrigou-Lagrange with the rather challenging title, *Priesthood and Perfection*. The Introduction quickly sets a certain tone:

> The poisonous errors in modern life are tending toward a complete dechristianization of society, a dechristianization which began in the sixteenth century with the rebirth of paganism and the reappearance of pagan pride and sensuality among Christians. This turning from Christ advanced another stage under Protestantism, which rejected the Holy Sacrifice of the Mass.[60]

Just like Chrysostom, Garrigou-Lagrange wanted to remind priests that the vocation to be holy follows on from service at the altar. That might suggest that a 'high' doctrine of priesthood is probably Catholic in character. There is, though, another voice insisting on the same truth, and it is not Catholic at all.

In 1652 George Herbert's *Countrey Parson* was published, nearly 20 years after his death. It was seen through the press by a man called Barnabas Oley, who provided a Preface. That was a bitter-sweet task, because the ministry that Herbert described and that Oley had shared had been destroyed. Under Cromwell's Commonwealth, the Church of England, its clergy and the services of the Book of Common Prayer lay under a ban. Oley had been deprived of not one but two benefices (he was a pluralist) and wrote out of despair.

> Gods sinking the Gates, his destroying the wals, his slighting the strong holds of Zion; his polluting the Kingdom, his swallowing the Palaces, his cutting off the Horn of Israel: Gods hating our Feasts, his abominating our Sabaoths, his loathing our Solemnities ... Gods forgetting his footstool, his abhorring his Sanctuary, his casting off his Altar.[61]

A very different, and Presbyterian, ministry was now in place in England and it too was thinking hard about character and identity. The same year that Herbert's book was published, the Worcestershire Voluntary Association of Ministers was formed, bringing together something like 70 ministers from the West Midlands and Oxfordshire. Among them was Richard Baxter, who would soon produce another book, which was to be every bit as famous as *The Countrey Parson*.

Baxter was brought up in Anglicanism. He was ordained deacon in 1638 (and was very probably made a priest soon after, but there is no record of it). He was also, however, someone who kept company with men and women on the borders of Anglican conformity. As the House of Commons set about first reforming and then later abolishing the Church of England, his star was suddenly in the ascendant and, in 1641, he accepted the post of Lecturer in Kidderminster. He made a bad beginning. Tempers were frayed and he got shouted at in the street. Fearing for his safety, he left and spent the years of 'war and flames' elsewhere. He was back in Kidderminster however, in the summer of 1647, and this time he stayed and resumed a remarkable ministry of writing, preaching (they had to add five galleries to the church to fit everyone in) and pastoral counselling.

It was hard work, but crowned with success.[62] Baxter saw something like 14 families in a week and began to think the Kingdom was coming: 'England had been like in a quarter of an age to have become a land of saints and a pattern of holiness to all the world, and an unmatchable paradise of the earth.'[63] Partially because he wished to commend his pastoral practice to others and partially because he always had a passionate attachment to what he called 'Christian concord', he became a key member of the Worcestershire Voluntary Association of Ministers. In 1655 he set out to 'draw all the ministers of the country' into following the Kidderminster model.[64] They agreed to meet at Worcester, in 1655, to pray and to commit themselves to the task, 'to join in humiliation and in earnest prayer to God, for the pardon of our neglects, and for his special assistance in the work which we had undertaken'.[65] Baxter was to preach.

In the event, he was too ill to attend his own party. Never a man to work in vain, the promised sermon was promptly worked up into a book, *The Reformed Pastor*. It was published in 1656. In one form or another it has not been out of print since. It was a sermon that he had originally planned, and so there was a text, Acts 20.28: 'Take heed therefore unto yourselves, and to all the flock, over the which the Holy Ghost hath made you overseers, to feed the church of God, which he hath purchased with his own blood.'

'Take heed therefore unto yourselves,' *The Reformed Pastor* begins by ramming the point home:

> Let us consider, what it is to take heed to ourselves.
> See that the work of saving grace be thoroughly wrought in your own souls. Take heed to yourselves, lest you be void of that saving grace of God which you offer to others.[66]

It was the point Gregory Nazianzus had grasped: you must not preach a holiness you do not practice. The work will not save you: 'Believe it, sirs, God is no respecter of persons: he saveth not men for their coats or callings; a holy calling will not save an unholy man.'[67] In *The Reformed Pastor* that point is made again and again. The minister who has no real holiness is like a tailor who goes in rags, or a cook who cannot even lick his fingers. It is a particular kind of horror: 'Oh what aggravated misery is this, to perish in the midst of plenty! – to famish with the bread of life in our hands, while we offer it to others, and urge it on them!'[68]

Assumptions about ministry were changing fast. In Presbyterian England there was a much greater emphasis on the language of individual calling. Congregations sought out their own ministers, as the people of Kidderminster sought out Baxter himself. They went looking for gifted men who could preach and teach. Ministry, suddenly, was all about action and personal authority. Baxter, who was almost ceaselessly active, had no quarrel with the culture of busy grace, but he was disturbed at what was happening to vocation. He was sure that all ministries began in saving faith, not in deeds of power. Candidates for ministry were in too much of a hurry. He thought too many men wanted to be 'preachers before they are Christians', 'and so to worship an unknown God, and to preach an unknown Christ, to pray through an unknown Spirit, to recommend a state of holiness and communion with God, and a glory and a happiness which are all unknown'.[69] Ministers preoccupied with their work, busy with particular challenges, missed the point. They would claim that a week was not long enough to prepare a sermon that would last an hour or two, but they failed to think at all about how they should live and behave for all those hours they were not in the pulpit: 'Oh how curiously have I heard some men preach; and how carelessly have I seen them live!'[70]

Baxter would have his minsters know God and attend to their lives. And then he would have them qualified too. They needed to know scripture and doctrine. They needed to know about sin and temptation. They needed to be strong and seasoned. Over and again Baxter returned to his text: 'Take heed to yourselves for you have a heaven to win or lose.' He was convinced that the devil singled out the clergy: 'He beareth the greatest malice to those that are engaged to do him the greatest mischief.'[71]

Like Chrysostom, Baxter worried about the temptations of office. Most subtle of all, perhaps, was the temptation just to act the part, to speak words of thunder against sin from the pulpit, but to speak in whispers out of it. Congregations would settle for that very happily.

They will give you leave to preach against their sins, and to talk as much as you will for godliness in the pulpit, if you will but let them alone afterwards, and be friendly and merry with them when you have done, and talk as they do, and live as they.

Richard Baxter knew that authenticity, a life that matched the rhetoric, was somewhere very near the heart of ministry.[72]

Preaching presented other challenges. Like other writers before, he noticed that good preachers begin to be more interested in whether people *liked* the sermon than in whether the sermon did its job. Pride 'goeth with us into the pulpit': 'When the sermon is done, pride goeth home with them, and maketh them more eager to know whether they were applauded, than whether they did prevail for the saving of souls.'[73] Pride also isolates us. With sharp insight, Baxter noticed that pride looks for reassurance, and when it does not find it assumes that silence is always hostility. The proud get locked into a desperate game of leapfrog, always discounting the last success in search of another. He noted other temptations too, observing that the clergy can be competitive with one another and also tempted to perform. He also described a temptation to be *secure*, a belief that only with more status or more possessions can we be effective. It is the seduction that has us forever doing the groundwork and never doing the job; buying books rather than writing sermons, making lists of people to visit without ever leaving the study.

'Take heed therefore unto yourselves'; there was no substitute for personal holiness. Yet Baxter was a realist. He did not set out the council of perfection you find in Gregory Nazianzus or Chrysostom. He wrote about concentrating on one place and on what might be done there.[74] That said, he expected the clergy to work hard. Driven to extraordinary effort himself, he reminded other ministers that it was unattractive to complain. No one is forced into ministry and if the work seems too much then look around for help. This was a view of ministry rooted in close experience of making disciples. He thought about the task and the tone of ministry. He knew the difference between a pastoral style that was serious and one that was cold. It is an important point. In ministry, manner matters – affection, courtesy, compassion open the door to grace.[75] Baxter thought ministers should model three virtues: ability, sincerity and unfeigned love.[76]

There was something sane and even pragmatic in Baxter's devoted and demanding ministry. Though he pushed himself so hard he knew that his aim was never excellence, it was always to do what was sufficient, good enough:

we must insist chiefly upon the greatest, most certain, and most necessary truths, and be more seldom and sparing upon the rest. If we can but teach Christ to our people, we shall teach them all. Get them well to heaven, and they will have knowledge enough ... I confess I think NECESSITY should be the great disposer of a minister's course of study and labour.[77]

It has to be said this was a particular kind of pragmatism. Baxter was not sure he could stay where the results did not follow, if he was to find himself among unprofitable people.[78] Of course, he understood perfectly well that the work was ultimately in God's hands not his. In that sense this was work that would not fail.

By your work you are related to Christ, as well as to the flock. You are the stewards of his mysteries, and rulers of his household; and he that entrusted you, will maintain you in his work ... Be true to him, and never doubt but he will be true to you.[79]

The Reformed Pastor ends with a description of Baxter's work in Kidderminster and a passionate appeal to others to take up the pattern of visiting and catechizing that he had adopted. He thought of ministry as relationship not performance.

It hath oft grieved my heart to observe some eminent able preachers, how little they do for the saving of souls, save only in the pulpit; and to how little purpose much of their labour is, by this neglect. They have hundreds of people that they never spoke a word to personally for their salvation.[80]

If we have not heard Baxter say this we have not understood him. His overriding concern was a ministry that touched individual lives, made a difference to what people thought and did. It did not count sermons preached or visits made; it looked always to lives transformed.

What have we our time and strength for, but to lay them out for God? What is a candle made for, but to burn? Burned and wasted we must be; and is it not fitter it should be in lighting men to heaven, and in working for God, than in living to the flesh?[81]

So, the book ends where it started, with the conviction that ministry is a way of life, rewarding, urgent and demanding complete commitment.

The lessons do not need labouring. Baxter, of all the writers we have met so far, has the surest eye for the temptation to hide in the role of priest. I have worked now, for several years, with a bishop who speaks of 'not drawing down status' from our role. He is on to something important. Ministry is a human office and our humanity must be on show. Vocation will shape character, but that is not the same thing as turning it into a role that must be played. Longing for generosity and tolerance, Baxter was shown little of either and was not only refused permission to serve as a curate in Kidderminster, he was forbidden to preach. That tested his patience beyond endurance and, subsequently, he was repeatedly prosecuted for preaching without licence; he had his books impounded and, aged 70, was imprisoned. The vision and hope that inspired *The Reformed Pastor* was dust and ashes, but Baxter's voice continues to insist steadily that at the heart of ministry there is a call to holiness.

Renew them in holiness

Immediately after the laying on of hands, the moment of ordination, a new priest hears the bishop pray over the newly ordained: 'Renew them in holiness.' Holiness is the expectation, and that holiness is a gift of grace. We do not talk about holiness in ministry very much. There are a number of reasons why that might be so. We are preoccupied by the need to be effective as we come to terms with a failure of evangelism. We are ashamed of the failings of the clergy who have been plastered over the press; we are rightly wary of suggesting that the ordained might be more holy than the laity; and we do not want to be unmasked as hypocrites. All that, and the added difficulty of the fact that we cannot agree what holiness looks like.

If there is any agreement at all among the authors described in this book it is that holiness, a particular kind of 'public holiness', is the basic characteristic of ministry in the Church. A ministry that lets slip the conviction that holiness is central is flawed and impoverished. Because holiness is such a challenge, because we fear its demands, because it finds us wanting, we are quick to settle for other assumptions about what ministry must be. The problem is that a ministry that sets preaching or counselling or professionalism or leadership at its heart sets that same assumption at the heart of the life of the Church. Then it is not just ministry that disappoints, but the body of Christ begins to look constrained.

Notes

1 H. P. Liddon, *Clerical Life and Work*, London: Longmans, 1897, p. 87.

2 Quoted in entry on Liddon in *Dictionary of National Biography*.

3 F. Higham, *Lancelot Andrewes*, London: SCM Press, 1952, p. 12; R. S. Thomas, *Autobiographies*, London: J. M. Dent, 1997, p. 59.

4 2 Kings 2.12.

5 Quoted in Desmond Morse-Boycott, *Lead Kindly Light: Studies of the Saints and Heroes of the Oxford Movement*, London: Centenary Press, 1932.

6 J. O. Johnston, *The Life and Letters of Henry Parry Liddon*, London: Longmans, Green & Co., 1904, p. 32.

7 Liddon's Notebook in the College Archive in Cuddesdon, VP 1/1 f.3.

8 *Cuddesdon College, 1854–1929: A Record and a Memorial*, Oxford: Oxford University Press, 1930.

9 H. P. Liddon, 'The Work and Prospects of Theological Colleges', a sermon preached at the Cuddesdon Anniversary Festival, 10 June 1868, printed in H. P. Liddon, *Clerical Life and Work*, London: Longmans, 1894, p. 52. Available online at http://anglicanhistory.org/liddon/cuddesdon1868.html.

10 Liddon, *Clerical Life and Work*, p. 58.

11 Liddon, *Clerical Life and Work*, p. 58.

12 Liddon, *Clerical Life and Work*, p. 62.

13 H. P. Liddon, 'The Priest in his Inner Life', published in *Clerical Life and Work*, p. 3.

14 Liddon, *Clerical Life and Work*, p. 4.

15 J. J. Blunt, 'Lectures on the Duties of a Parish Priest', quoted in *Clerical Life and Work*, pp. 1, 2.

16 Liddon, *Clerical Life and Work*, pp. 22–3.

17 Liddon, *Clerical Life and Work*, p. 103.

18 Liddon, *Clerical Life and Work*, p. 128.

19 Liddon, *Clerical Life and Work*, pp. 129, 130.

20 Liddon, *Clerical Life and Work*, p. 264.

21 Liddon, *Clerical Life and Work*, p. 265.

22 Ordination of Priests, Book of Common Prayer.

23 Liddon, *Clerical Life and Work*, p. 263.

24 B. E. Daley, *Gregory of Nazianzus*, Abingdon: Routledge, 2006, p. 9.

25 A. Meredith, *The Cappadocians*, London: Geoffrey Chapman, 1995, p. 2.

26 Gregory of Nazianzus, *Oration* 2, 'In Defence of his Flight to Pontus', 1, trans. E. Hamilton Gifford, *N&PNF 2S*, 7.

27 Gregory of Nazianzus, *Oration* 2, 6.

28 Gregory of Nazianzus, *Oration* 2, 6.

29 Gregory of Nazianzus, *Oration* 2, 8.

30 Exodus 4.1; 4.10; 4.13; 4.14.

31 Isaiah 6.5.

32 Luke 5.8.

33 Gregory of Nazianzus, *Oration* 2, 12.

34 Gregory of Nazianzus, *Oration* 2, 13.

35 Gregory of Nazianzus, *Oration* 2, 22.

36 R. Hooker, *Of the Laws of Ecclesiastical Polity*, 5.77.1, 2, 10, in J. Keble (ed.), *The Works of … Richard Hooker*, Oxford: Clarendon Press, 1865.

37 G. Herbert, 'The Priesthood', in F. E. Hutchinson (ed.), *The Works of George Herbert*, Oxford: Clarendon Press, 1953, p.160.

38 K. Mason, *Priesthood and Society*, Norwich: Canterbury Press, 2002, pp. 13, 17.

39 Mason, *Priesthood and Society*, p. 1.

40 Gregory of Nazianzus, *Oration* 2, 3

41 Gregory of Nazianzus, *Oration* 2, 22

42 Gregory of Nazianzus, *Oration* 2, 24.

43 Gregory of Nazianzus, *Oration* 2, 39.

44 Gregory of Nazianzus, *Oration* 2, 71.

45 Gregory of Nazianzus, *Oration* 2, 9.

46 John Chrysostom, *On the Priesthood* I.6, in P. Schaff and H. Wace (ed.), *A Select Library of the Nicene and Post-Nicene Fathers of the Christian Church* (NPNF), New York and Oxford: 1886–89, 1 09, pp. 34–5, and *Introduction*, pp. 28–9.

47 John Chrysostom, *On the Priesthood* 1.1ff.

48 R. A. Krupp, *Shepherding the Flock of God*, New York: Peter Lang, 1991, p. 1.

49 J. N. D. Kelly, *Golden Mouth*, Ithaca, NY: Cornell University Press, 1995, p. 27; A. Hofer, *Christ in the Life and Teaching of Gregory of Nazianzus*, Oxford: Oxford University Press, 2013, p. 199.

50 Clement First Epistle 42; see below, p. 134.

51 John Chrysostom, *On the Priesthood* 2.2.

52 John Chrysostom, *On the Priesthood* 2.2.

53 Ephesians 6.12.

54 John Chrysostom, *On the Priesthood* 3.4.

55 John Chrysostom, *On the Priesthood* 3.5.

56 John Chrysostom, *On the Priesthood* 3.14.

57 John Chrysostom, *On the Priesthood* 3.9.

58 John 21.20–21.

59 E. Dickinson, 'The Only News I Know'.

60 R. Garrigou-Lagrange OP, *The Priesthood and Perfection*, trans. E. Hayden, Westminster MD: The Newman Press, 1955, 'Introduction'.

61 B. Oley, 'A Prefatory View of the Life and Vertues of the Authour, and Excellencies of This Book', in *Herbert's Remains. Or, Sundry Pieces Of that sweet Singer of the Temple, Mr. George Herbert* (London: 1652), reprinted in R. H. Ray, 'The Herbert Allusion Book', *Studies in Philology*, LXXXIII (Fall 1986), pp. 40–6, at p. 41.

62 R. Baxter, *The Reformed Pastor*, II.I.1.9, Edinburgh: Banner of Truth, 1974, pp. 183–4. You can also find *The Reformed Pastor* online at www.reformed.org/books/baxter/reformed_pastor.

63 *The Autobiography of Richard Baxter*, ed. N. H. Keeble, London: Dent, 1974, p. 84.

64 *Autobiography of Richard Baxter*, p. 97.

65 Baxter, *The Reformed Pastor*, 'Dedication', p. 37.

66 Baxter, *The Reformed Pastor*, I.1.1, p. 53.

67 Baxter, *The Reformed Pastor*, I.2.1, p. 73.

68 Baxter, *The Reformed Pastor*, I.2.1, pp. 54–5.

69 Baxter, *The Reformed Pastor*, I.2.1, p. 56.

70 Baxter, *The Reformed Pastor*, I.1.3, p. 64.

71 Baxter, *The Reformed Pastor*, I.2.3, p. 74.

72 Baxter, *The Reformed Pastor*, I.2.8(4), p. 85.

73 Baxter, *The Reformed Pastor*, III.1.1, p. 138.

74 Baxter, *The Reformed Pastor*, II.1.2, p. 88.

75 A point made by John Drury, *The Burning Bush*, London: Fount, 1990, p. 13.

76 Baxter, *The Reformed Pastor*, III.2.3, p. 232.

77 Baxter, *The Reformed Pastor*, II.2.4, p. 113.

78 Baxter, *The Reformed Pastor*, II.2.13, p. 121.

79 Baxter, *The Reformed Pastor*, II.3.1(5), pp. 128–9.

80 Baxter, *The Reformed Pastor*, III.2.1.7, p. 178.

81 Baxter, *The Reformed Pastor*, III.2.2, Objection 4(4), p. 218.

8

Gifts in Ministry

Living with variety

The Church is a body that has Christ as its head; it is a chosen people, a royal priesthood; it is God's vineyard, God's building, and it is the bride of Christ.[1] Strange then, that life in this glorious community is all too often bad-tempered, frustrating and downright unkind. Christians keep falling out with one another. There are days when it seems that falling out is what we do best. And, when we do fall out, it seems, just as the *Didache* suggests, that the ministry of the Church is more often part of the problem than part of the solution. Our difficulty is the problem that we keep having with *gifts*.

Ministry is a gift; minsters are gifted people. When St Paul describes ministry he insists on two points. First, ministry is various, it might be healing, it might be prophecy, or it might be the utterance of wisdom. So, I will minister in one way and you will minister in quite another. Second, that difference between us exists because we are differently gifted. Paul insists that ministry is a gift of the Spirit.[2] Now, gifts are splendid; the whole business of giving gifts and getting gifts can be really delightful. The problem is that gifts are also specific, particular; you get one thing and I get another. At Christmas, I might just occasionally struggle with the guilty recognition that I am jealous because someone else has just been given what I want. And then I might struggle all over again if someone else does not seem grateful for the gift I have given. In Paul's epistles, some are prophets, but most are not; some people have gifts of healing, but most do not. Gifts can bring us closer, but they can also push us apart.

My call to ministry began with a rather vague sense of what the clergy do and, if I am honest, with the inspiration provided by a man I admired. What followed was the slow business of working out what that vocation meant for me, and learning that I must not long for something else, nor try to be something I am not. It is still work in progress.

> Like the novice in the desert, I must watch the elders and learn the shape and the rhythm of being Christian from those who have walked further and worked harder; but then I have to take my own steps, and create a life that has never been lived before.[3]

The truth is that it can be hard for some of us to enjoy ourselves; hard for us to take pleasure in the business of really *being* ourselves. Dithering over being more accommodating or more assertive, and struggling with the push-me–pull-you demands of ambition and exhaustion is bad enough. When we raise our eyes from the mirror it can actually get worse and we become acutely aware that some other people are making an impressive and attractive job of being quite different from us. Making the most of our own gifts is a challenge; admiring other people's gifts can be a real trial. So, in a world full of gifts, some of us have a problem with envy. We keep taking our eyes off what we have been given, in order to wonder whether someone else hasn't done rather better. In Marilynne Robinson's book *Gilead*, an elderly priest writes a memoir and ruefully admits that 'covetise' has been the curse of his ministry. Among all the Commandments, he has struggled most with the insistence, in the tenth, that we must not covet:

> I believe the sin of covetise is that pang of resentment you may feel when even the people you love best have what you want and don't have. From the point of view of loving your neighbour as yourself (Leviticus 19:18), there is nothing that makes a person's fallenness more undeniable than covetise – you feel it right in your heart, in your bones … 'Rejoice with those who rejoice.' I have found that difficult too often. I was much better at weeping with those who weep.[4]

Called into fullness of life, we struggle. As the Epistle to the Ephesians explains, our vocation is to grow to full maturity, 'to the measure of the full stature of Christ'.[5] Christianity is just a call to live the life of Christ; live as he lived, where you live, as you live. There is no special knowledge, no trick to learn, no secret handshake. You can't pass exams, you can't check the handbook, and you can't complete a process. Because there is no formula, we will each live in Christ in different ways. Then we fall out, because we are selfish and insecure, and struggle to celebrate the way other people live differently from us. Secretly, some of us would like everyone else to admire *our* way of being human and wish they were not quite so successful in their way. Of course, it is a great blessing that we are distinctively gifted. It gets us out of the hall of mirrors, and yet we keep experiencing it as a challenge and a problem. Belonging to an order, being a communion, living in the one body, is much harder than we sometimes admit.

Clement, the problem of envy

Our flair for falling out with one another has always been a challenge. It raises its head in one of the earliest documents we have. The letter of Clement of Rome is, like the *Didache*, difficult to date precisely. It was probably written about 95–96 CE, though some have suggested it is earlier than that. Written by Clement, who was Bishop of Rome, it is a letter addressed to the church in Corinth. At the time of writing, the problem of disunity in Corinth (which had so exercised St Paul) had become a scandal. Clement wrote about 'that shameful and detestable sedition, utterly abhorrent to the elect of God'.[6] The only clues as to what was causing the Corinthians to squabble are in the letter itself and, as Clement adopted the rather lofty approach of someone who does not want to grub about in the detail, we are not told very much. That said, we can be fairly sure that they were arguing, as they had argued before, about leadership and spiritual authority. They were arguing, in short, about their priests.

It is disgraceful, beloved, yea, highly disgraceful, and un-
worthy of your Christian profession, that such a thing should
be heard of as that the most steadfast and ancient Church of
the Corinthians should, on account of one or two persons,
engage in sedition against its presbyters.[7]

In Corinth, it seems a few lay people were challenging their
presbyters and competing for their role: 'and their own proper
place is prescribed to the priests ... The layman is bound by the
laws that pertain to laymen.'[8] Part of the problem was clearly
a contest over status, power and who had the right to do what.
It was, in short, jealousy and insecurity. That is what Clement
wrote about, confusion and competition in the Church. He
urged people to find their proper place, suggested that each
Corinthian would do well to consider 'not going beyond the
rule of the ministry prescribed to him'.[9] Clement recognized,
however, that the real enemy was not a debate about hierarchy,
but sheer, bad-tempered ill will, what Clement called 'envy'.

To deal with this crisis, Clement had four things to say.
First, he argued that envy was lethal and schism and discord
a disgrace. Second, he suggested that humility, hospitality and
love were the proper virtues that we should practice. Third,
he argued that good order is what God gave us in creation.[10]
Then, fourth and finally, Clement addressed the issue of particular ministries. God, he said, is a God of providence; God
has a purpose. So, God sent forth Christ and Christ sent forth
the apostles 'in an orderly way'. We should notice, in passing, that Clement thinks that when we talk about ministry, we
should talk about behaviour, doctrine and order. Those are the
headlines. Ministry draws its character and identity from principle, not practice. We also need to notice that Clement took a
critical step. He did not simply say that Christ called apostles,
he went on to argue that the apostles then made a further set
of appointments:

Having therefore received their orders ... they went forth
proclaiming that the kingdom of God was at hand. And thus
preaching through countries and cities, they appointed the

first-fruits [of their labours], having first proved them by the Spirit, to be bishops and deacons of those who should afterwards believe.[11]

In the *Didache*, remember, there was an uneasy relationship between apostles and the ministers you might find in a particular place. Apostles are itinerant, blown by the Spirit from place to place; bishops are local. There was no suggestion, in the *Didache*, that the way to tidy up the confusion between these different callings was to regard bishops as *successors* to the apostles, nor to think of them as having been appointed *by* the apostles. In fact, the *Didache* tells us that it is the job of the local church to secure for itself a local ministry: 'Appoint, therefore, for yourselves, bishops and deacons.'[12] In Clement's hands the story changes. Suddenly bishops and deacons are described as having their origins in divine providence, not local election. Their commission comes, he argued, from Christ, via the apostles. It was neat and tidy, it solved a problem and became a theological commonplace; we have met it already in the work of Charles Gore.[13] Clement himself, however, felt the need to work hard, even frantically, to justify his argument. He suggested that God's intention to create sacred ministers can be traced back deep into scripture and he calls Isaiah as a witness: 'I will appoint their bishops in righteousness, and their deacons in faith.' The difficulty of this, of course, as footnotes often rather laconically point out, is that 'the text here is altered by Clement'. What the Septuagint version of Isaiah actually says is, 'I will give thy rulers in peace and thy overseers in righteousness.'[14] There is nothing at all there about bishops, or deacons. Clement also drew on the story of Aaron's staff in Numbers 17, a story in which God both blessed a particular ministry and punished those who had opposed it.[15] Clement was perhaps a little less genteel than he sounded. Any attempt to challenge the ordained ministry was apparently an act of defiance to God and to the commission given to the apostles by Christ himself, and in Clement's mind it would not go unpunished.

So, the *Epistle of Clement* gave bishops, presbyters and deacons apostolic origins. His work was a landmark for our understanding of ministry and one of the points at which our sense of hierarchy was developed. It was a fork in the journey. If you think apostolicity is what defines ministry you might think some ministries are more apostolic than others and then assume that they must have privilege and status. If you think ministry begins in the baptism we all share, you will come to a different conclusion. Because this argument is controversial it is important to attend to it, but we must not get distracted from the real thrust of what Clement had to say.

Like St Paul, Clement was fundamentally concerned with the problem of gifts. The Corinthian church was stuffed full of gifted men and women. And, as anyone who has ever lived in a smart street, in a smart district will tell you, gifted and charismatic people may be good leaders, but they can be poor neighbours. Corinth was a city with too many chiefs. St Clement knew the Corinthians and their strengths: 'Every kind of honour and happiness was bestowed upon you.'[16] He was well aware that they were gifted and knew the scriptures. He was also sure that with great gifts come great temptations: 'You see, brethren, that the greater the knowledge that has been vouchsafed to us, the greater also is the danger to which we are exposed.'[17] Then Clement twists the knife. He tells the Corinthians that the gifts of which they are so proud, the gifts which form the basis of their competition for office, for dignity and for power, mislead them. Gifts are the things we get even though we do not deserve them. Gifts do not confer status; they remind us that we are needy. 'For what can a mortal man do? or what strength is there in one made out of the dust?'[18] We may be gifted, but all we can offer to God are things that God has given us.

Clement reminded us that all gifts and callings have their origin in God. No one individual commands respect because of a particular calling. We are all called. And if that is true it is only in the complete concert of gifts that there is real beauty and dignity. 'The great cannot subsist without the small, nor the small without the great. There is a kind of mixture in all things, and thence arises mutual advantage.'[19]

Gifts come and go, and we miss the point if we prioritize

a few. All these gifts are supposed to fit together. We are meant to be a gifted community. We are meant to enjoy the heady variety of it. In Christ we do not celebrate ourselves, but one another. In *The Christlike God*, John V. Taylor memorably quoted a story-poem by Charles Williams, in which a 'gentleman of quality' is asked to the Prince Emmanuel's ball, but is horrified to see that it is 'fancy dress'. His motto is 'I always strive to be myself'. Because he is a friend of the Prince Emmanuel, he decides that an exception will be made for him. He duly arrives at the ball and tries to get in; his way is barred by a footman with exquisite manners. Indeed the footman is altogether exquisite, wearing dazzling livery and dropping shafts of light. He has come to the gate of heaven and angels surround him. With no fancy dress, he is denied admission. Instead, the angel stands aside and lets him glimpse the hall where everyone is indeed in dress other than their own:

> This guest his brother's courage wore;
> that, his wife's zeal, while, just before,
> she in his steady patience shone;
> there a young lover had put on
> the fine integrity of sense
> his mistress used; magnificence
> a father borrowed of his son,
> who was not there ashamed to don
> his father's wise economy.
> No he or she was he or she
> merely; no single being dared,
> except the Angels of the Guard,
> come without other kind of dress
> than this poor life had to profess.[20]

The gentleman of quality is shut out, not for wanting to be himself, but for only wanting that. We are called to be ourselves and to be together. We are called to acknowledge, day after day, that ministry is plural.

Clement believed in interdependence and knew that envy is insidious and deadly. He knew that we have to fit the pieces together. He insisted that good order is not just important, it is fundamental. In fact he believed that there is an order that is God-given, an order that can be read off from creation which 'the great Creator and Lord of all has appointed to exist in peace and harmony'. This same order needs to be seen in the Church. It is the task of the clergy, argued Clement, to help us arrange our gifts in order. That is an insight that has informed our understanding of church structure and of ordained ministry – the ministry of *orders* – ever since.

It has to be said, Clement's enthusiastic account of a God-given order can be a bit of a challenge. He saw patterns and peace where, often, we see chaos and terror.[21] Even so, he made an important theological point. The creation stories in Genesis offer the fundamental insight that God brings order out of chaos. One thing is divided from another, but a pattern emerges. Light was separated from dark, waters from land, and so on. Creation is a great celebration of the way one thing differs from another and of the relationship between all things that are made. Theologians and artists have routinely celebrated the fact that God is a God of order, proportion, harmony and resolution.

Each morning in Gloucester Cathedral, Morning Prayer is said in a small stone chapel built by Norman masons. The chapel is dominated by a stunning modern window made by a Gloucestershire artist called Thomas Denny. At first glance it looks like an abstract study in shades of blue, but closer inspection tells a different story. The central panel shows the encounter between Thomas and the risen Christ; either side is a meditation on Psalm 148.

Praise the LORD from the earth, you sea monsters and all deeps, fire and hail, snow and frost, stormy wind fulfilling his command! Mountains and all hills, fruit trees and all cedars! Wild animals and all cattle, creeping things and flying birds![22]

The window is rich and various, but it is not chaotic. Here is the work of a God who orders creation, but makes it various.

You can have order without uniformity. That is how the New Testament understands ministry. The Epistle to the Ephesians insists different God-given gifts work together for the common good:

> The gifts he gave were that some would be apostles, some prophets, some evangelists, some pastors and teachers, to equip the saints for the work of ministry, for building up the body of Christ, until all of us come to the unity of the faith and of the knowledge of the Son of God, to maturity, to the measure of the full stature of Christ.[23]

The Church is the theatre in which variety is ordered. It is the task of the ministry of the Church to sustain that order. The new Introduction to the *Common Worship: Ordination Services* says as much: 'The whole body of the Church is ordered in faithful response to the Lord's summons to share his work' (p. 4). Ordained ministers have the privilege and challenge of holding together the great concert of gifts.

Clement asserted both the particularity and the dignity of priesthood. He gave it a back story and urged the importance of order. Too often we have let the stress fall on the boldness of his claims and read Clement (as we have read other authors, like Cyprian) just so that we can be thrilled and impressed by the sheer dignity of priesthood. That legacy has been a burden to the Church; one ministry shouldering out all others. Priesthood properly exists precisely in order that this should never happen. All of us, and priests in particular, need to be less impressed by what a few good people have already done and much more excited about what the whole Church might become when all the gifts of God are freed. Priests must learn the lesson that Clement taught, that the heart of ministry is humility. We all know that the Kingdom is not a community of strong characters braying out their success. We are quick to notice and quick to dismiss priests who are merely pompous. It is a more subtle challenge that leads us astray. Within a generation the once unassailable status of all the professions has taken a tumble. In the same period, there has been a still more startling shift in perceptions of the clergy, who are no longer regarded as socially significant and have had to endure the disgrace that falls on all following the terrible crimes of a few. The clergy are left examining the shreds of reputation at precisely the same time as many of them have lost their association with a community because they have become vicar of three, four or five parishes. The clergy are left renegotiating questions about their status and role. Meanwhile, a renewed sense that the challenges facing the Church call for strong leadership issues out in a conviction that the clergy might need to impose themselves afresh and quickly. Loss of status and change of status have bred anxiety, stress and competition. Priests become envious of other leaders and are too easily threatened by one another, or just fascinated by their own reflection. It is precisely at this moment that we forget that we are supposed to celebrate diversity and call it into unity. We look for heroes when we should be looking for each other.

Michael Ramsey

In 1961 Ramsey succeeded Geoffrey Fisher and became the one hundredth Archbishop of Canterbury. As he waited to complete the move to Lambeth, he gave a television interview and spoke about what lay ahead:

> People ask me, sometimes, if I am in good heart about being Archbishop ... My answer is 'Yes' ... But the phrase 'in good heart', gives me pause, because after all, we are here as a church to represent Christ crucified and the compassion of Christ crucified before the world. And, because that is so, it may be the will of God that our church should have its heart broken and perhaps the heart of its Archbishop broken with it.[24]

'We are here as a church to represent Christ crucified and the compassion of Christ crucified': that is as good a summary of Ramsey's theology of ministry as you can get. Before we pick up the little book on ministry that he wrote, it really helps to understand the deep convictions that inform it.

Earlier in his career, while he was teaching at the theological college in Lincoln, in 1936, Ramsey published *The Gospel and the Catholic Church*.[25] At the very beginning of the book he acknowledged a problem: 'the first need of the Christians in face of the apathy and the bewilderment about the Church, is to know and to be able to say plainly what the Church really is'.[26] Ramsey could answer that question; he knew exactly what the Church really is. The Church is the death and resurrection of Jesus Christ: 'We are here as a church to represent Christ crucified and the compassion of Christ crucified.'

Christ's passion is the foundation of the Church and its ministry. Ramsey's books insist on the centrality of the passion of Christ and our own vocation to die that we might live. We would fundamentally misunderstand him, however, if we read that and assumed his outlook was pessimistic or life-denying. Beneath and beyond the commitment to the passion there is another element to Ramsey's theology. He had a lot to say about glory, and he always had an eye to what the Church would one day become. That future was a mystery to him; it is a mystery to us all. As St John puts it, 'what we will be has not yet been revealed'.[27] Nonetheless, Ramsey knew that a vocation to wear a crown of thorns would lead, inevitably, through resurrection, to a crown of glory.

So, 'the Cross is the place where the theology of the Church has its meaning'.[28] Ramsey's argument was rooted in scripture and littered with biblical reference. We have a church only because Christ 'gave himself up for her' and have unity only because strangers have been reconciled 'in his fleshly body through death'. [29] The Church takes its identity not from the fact that Christ lived, but from the fact that he died. Our worship proclaims that truth: 'For as often as you eat this bread and drink the cup, you proclaim the Lord's death until he comes.'[30] These are very familiar phrases. We know that Paul chose to know nothing 'except Jesus Christ and him crucified'.[31] We must not allow this familiarity to blind us to the startling truth that Ramsey set out. The Church is not a group of people who have heard about the death of Christ. It is not even a community created by Christ dying. The Church, Ramsey argues, *is* the death of Christ. The whole story of God's providence and love is contained in one individual and perfectly expressed in his death. The story of Israel is a massive epic, but in scripture the telescope keeps getting turned round and the whole is summed up in the one. The one man dying on the cross is, paradoxically, a nation; he is the Israel of God. Then that story becomes our story as we are baptized into his death and discover that we can only have 'a life of which crucifixion is a quality, a life of living through dying'.[32]

It follows that the Church does not start when Jesus and one other person get united to form a new community and then add others to their ranks. The Church is a community that exists in Christ even as he dies alone; *he* is the whole people of God. Joining ourselves to Christ, we get added into the community he contains. Once you get hold of this idea that the Church is the death of Christ and the death of Christ is a glimpse of God, you finally shake off the idea that there is something you need to bring, something you need to add. The Church is already complete. The Christian vocation really does not turn on making an effort and improving things. Christian identity is inclusion in Christ. Christ shares our death so that we can share his death and then share in his resurrection too. As Ramsey puts it: 'One died for all, therefore all died. To say this is to describe the Church of God.'[33] It is the great claim of Christians that they are 'in Christ'. Reading Ramsey, we begin to see what it means to be 'in Christ' and to understand more clearly how his life and death define us.

> Christianity therefore is never solitary. It is never true to say that separate persons are united to Christ, and then combine to form the Church; for to believe in Christ is to believe in One whose Body is a part of Himself and whose people are His own humanity, and to be joined to Christ is to be joined to Christ-in-his Body.[34]

Ramsey breathed fire into words that we use too freely. If I write a book and it sits on a shelf, or if someone takes a photograph of me and stuffs the picture in a drawer, then there are, in different places, things that are associated with me. My body, though, is different; where my body is, I am fully *there*. When we talk about the Church as the *body of Christ* that is what Ramsey meant. Christians together are Christ's body. They are not associated with him, or linked to him, they are indistinguishable from him; their lives make his humanity visible. Understand this and we understand the conviction that drove the sermons that make up *The Christian Priest Today*. When we know that the theology matters as much as this we can see why he wants the clergy to be theologians. When we know that our disunity actually breaks Christ's body all over again, we know why reconciliation matters so much to him.

Ramsey's abiding commitment to the unity of the Church shaped his own work as archbishop and what he has to say about ministry more generally. Unity is not an ambition, it is an identity. The Church has to express its one identity in what it does and says.

> The whole structure of the Church tells of the Gospel; not only by its graces and virtues, but also by its mere organic shape it proclaims the truth. A Baptism, a Eucharistic service, an Apostle, in themselves tell us of our death and resurrection and of the Body which is one.[35]

So, certain services and certain ministries are the marks of *order*. That order matters more than any individual. Order takes precedence over the flashy gifts of individuals and trumps all our priorities. This is what the Corinthians had to learn; it is why St Paul wrote to them so passionately urging them to become the Church and to stop celebrating themselves. Christianity is not a matter of being gifted and talented, it is learning dependence. What gifts we do have, have no use at all if we are not part of the one body.

The 'order' of ministry reminds us of our unity in Christ's passion. The job of an ordained minister is, quite simply, to remind the Church of this identity. The clergy are there to make us one in Christ, make us into the Church. As Ramsey put it:

> Today the ordained priest is called to reflect the priesthood of Christ and to serve the priesthood of the people of God, and to be one of the means of grace whereby God enables the Church to be the Church.[36]

Clement longed for unity and tried to make it official; claiming that bishops were appointed by Christ, he insisted on the importance of certain *offices*. Ramsey knew the argument, but was not interested in pursuing catholic conviction down the narrow, gothic corridors of clericalism. The question that interested him was not whether Christ himself commanded a particular kind of church structure, but rather whether the structure we have inherited, with its bishops, presbyters and deacons, can properly speak of the one gospel and one body. He did not describe a ministry that could impose itself on the Church because it had authority. He described a ministry that spoke to the Church of its true identity. Ministry, like all the other marks of the Church, and all Christian gifts, is worthless apart from the body.

> All who are baptised into Christ are members of his Church, and Baptism is the first mark of churchmanship. Yet the growth of all Christians into the measure of the stature of the fullness of Christ means their growth with all the saints in the unity of the one Body, and of this unity the Episcopate is the expression ... It proclaims that there is one family of god before and behind them all, and that all die daily in the Body of Him who dies and rose.[37]

Ministry for Ramsey was a summons into Christ's death. That is a lesson that generations of clergy have learned from him without perhaps ever quite grasping it. Ramsey's book *The Christian Priest Today* was published in 1972. More than 40 years later, it is this book that ordinands will tell you that they have read. It is still in print, or you can pick up copies in second-hand bookshops, and find pencil markings in the margins where the priest, whose name is written small on the flyleaf (often with the date and the name of the retreat house where the book was bought) has taken hold of the lessons to be learnt. The book is a collection of ordination charges and sets out the beliefs that we have just rehearsed. So, here we will find Ramsey urging the clergy to preach the message 'die to live':

> *Die to live.* Here too is the meaning of the Church, and the meaning of apostolic ministry: 'always bearing about in the body the dying of Jesus, that the life also of Jesus may be manifested in our body'.[38]

Perhaps the most famous and familiar charge is the first in the book. It establishes that the relationships that matter are not just with members of the congregation. Ramsey argues that there are four functions of the ministry of priests. First, the priest should be a *person of theology*. What he means is that priests should have studied in such a way that they can make their teaching simple. They should speak out of understanding. Their theology will not be abstract and remote, it will be done in partnership, bringing divine truth into the contemporary world, listening to what others have to say, and making connections. Theology is not the pursuit of learning, it is the greater challenge of finding the right words.

Second, a priest should be a *minister of reconciliation*. That is not a theological way of saying that the clergy should tell people to be nice to one another. Ramsey was suggesting that the clergy should remember that they minister the reconciliation that Christ won on Calvary. They should speak of the reality of sin and being forgiven and restored people in the love of God and of each other. Any relationship can only be born out of forgiveness.

The third function of priesthood is that a priest should be a *person of prayer*, praying theology into the parish, praying (as a sinner) for him- or herself, and for others. This praying is more than saying the words; it is itself a relationship. Ramsey pointed out that Jesus prayed and prays still. The text from which the address springs is taken from Hebrews: 'he always lives to make intercession for them' (Hebrews 7.25). Ramsey explains that the verb we translate as 'intercede' doesn't mean 'make petitions for'; it means *meet* or *encounter*. Jesus doesn't just 'say' prayers, Ramsey told us:

> Jesus is *with* the Father; with him in the intimate response of perfect humanity, with him in the power of Calvary and Easter; with him as one who bears us all upon his heart, our Son of Man, our friend, our priest; with him as our own.[39]

When Jesus prays he is with us, and with the Father, bringing us together. And that is how we are to pray as deacons and priests. As Ramsey put it 'To be with God with the people on our heart'.

Prayer is not simply the associations we can make or the bridges we can build in our minds; prayer is a meeting with Christ, a share in what he shares with the Father and the Spirit. The prayer of the clergy is a prayer for the unity of the Church and for our unity in Christ, bringing together people, God and priests. Theology, reconciliation and prayer are the tools that Ramsey believed could offer the hope of unity in a divided world and in parishes where experience and aspiration constantly pull people apart.

Ramsey, though, has not finished. Finally, the priest is a *person of the Eucharist*, praying the prayer of the Church in every age, bringing together the past and the future. In praying the Eucharist, priests help people to see that they are not just called to a common meal, but draw near to Calvary and the broken body and the spilt blood. The Eucharist confronts the Church with its own identity, the passion of Christ. 'In the Eucharist it proclaims Christ's death and feeds upon his life.'[40]

Ramsey was a shy and introverted man, but *The Christian Priest Today* is forged from the assumption that we live out faith in company. He also knew ministry was not just principle, it was experience, it was emotional. He preached on the gospel set in the Book of Common Prayer for the ordination of deacons: Luke 12.35–46, 'Blessed are those servants, whom the Lord when he cometh shall find watching.' He said this:

> Think of your ministry as a series of comings of Christ ...
> How does he come? In times of your grief and disappoint-
> ment he comes ... In times of joy in your ministry he comes ...
> And in times of your complacency or unfaithfulness he comes
> ... Watch and be ready.

That is the first consequence of ministry, the promise, the
challenge and the risk of Christ being close at hand. The
second consequence is the roller coaster of emotion hinted
at in that quotation: grief, disappointment and joy. Ramsey
was convinced that there was delight to be taken in ministry.
The addresses and charges speak repeatedly of 'the joy of the
priest'. There is joy to be had in seeing life in rich variety and
joy in watching the grace of God at work.[41] He also knew that
there were disappointments. He wrote about those as if he
knew them well:

> There is fatigue of body and mind. There can be worries
> about home and family. There is the monotony of times when
> the spark seems to go out and every day seems grey, damp
> and foggy and there comes the spiritual listlessness the monks
> call *accidie*, a mood of lazy depression.[42]

In both sorrow and joy Ramsey would have the clergy remember that they (like the whole Church of God) share in the life of
Christ and that Christ himself summoned us to joy and sorrow.
Priests should expect their share in Christ's suffering not as ele-
vated mystical experience, but in the routine of daily ministry.

Close to Christ's coming, knowing joy and sorrow as a
share in Christ's life, priests are inevitably tempted to take
themselves too seriously and are easily beguiled by their own
dignity. Sadly, jealousy of others is another threat and priests
can spend too long admiring or condemning their neighbours
without realizing the real damage they do is to themselves. So,
in Ramsey as in Clement, there is a constant reminder about
the call to humility:

> Run a good parish, preach a good sermon, carry out a suc-
> cessful project, do a worthwhile piece of work; and you are

pleased and happy. But this will not become the pleasure of pride and self-esteem if you are sharing in the joy of Jesus that his work is being done and people are being brought to him.[43]

Humility is an essential quality. There is only one kind of person who makes God known and realized by other people, and that is the person who is humble because he or she knows God, and knows God because he or she is humble.[44]

Ministry, then, can never be an achievement.

Telling the whole truth

Priests, Ramsey argued, pay attention, they see the world as it is and the Church as it is, and tell the truth about both. In part, in their work of teaching and preaching, in prayer and in the ministry of reconciliation, priests read the signs of the times and interpret them. They tell the truth in order to summon us to be what we should be. Rowan Williams puts it like this:

> There has to be in every priest just a bit of the poet and artist – enough to keep alive a distaste for nonsense, cheapness of words and ideas, stale and predictable reactions. And this is a crucial part of being visibly a sign of what and where the Church is, the Church which is called to live 'in' the truth.[45]

It is for this reason that priests need to be theologians. Not in order to write essays, or preach sermons that need footnotes, nor even to talk about eschatology over coffee and biscuits at meetings of the deanery chapter. The clergy need to be theologians so that they can put the gospel into words and describe our common Christian vocation here and now. We are not well served by those who make it complicated, or by those who tell us that it is beautiful and mysterious, or (worst of all) tell us that theology is not relevant. When we face crisis, when we feel the need to be urgent and decisive, we must not lose our distaste for nonsense and must not become predictable. We need clergy who know that the Church is not a building or a group of people; it is not something we do, or a community we make. The Church is the passion of Christ and the presence and the power of God. The Church is also our future; it is what we should become. We need priests who know that, priests who will never forget it.

We also need a theology that will unite us. The stress in our conversations currently falls, too often, on telling only part of the truth. I tell my story, you tell yours. It is the differences between us that fascinate. There is too little stress on our common humanity and our shared future. Struggling to describe the diversity all around us, we are often overwhelmed long before we begin to see the things that unite us. We then too quickly assume that the truth will always divide us. Rowan Williams, weathering the storms in a divided communion, had good reason to know just how difficult our divisions have become.

> The role of lookout is complex when our culture is simply so diverse, and when we are constantly struggling with a climate of pervasive mild cynicism, where the corruption of a lot of our communication leaves you feeling very much at sea in trying to find words of transparent truthfulness. The interpreter's job is a nightmare when Christians are sometimes positively eager to conclude that they have nothing to say to each other. The weaver may feel his or her integrity disappearing in the effort to create a living web of generous relationship, because we are all these days so much more self-aware, in sometimes less than helpful ways, aware of how we are seen and 'read' by others, and of the muddle of our own motivation.[46]

In the course of writing this book I began the work of a dean in an English cathedral. It is the job of the bishop to remind us of our unity in Christ. It is my job, with the help of my colleagues, to make that unity a reality at services like the Chrism Eucharist and ordinations. As the worship of the cathedral and its musical tradition become less and less familiar to many Christians, and the variety of practice in our parish churches grows, we have struggled to offer the diocese an experience we can all share. Preaching in parishes across the diocese I have been welcomed with great generosity of spirit into communities who have Christ at their heart, and yet I have felt a stranger because words and practice have been so unfamiliar. We are struggling to contain our own diversity, and we are struggling partly because experience is trumping reflection. We are not as interested as we should be in the theological expression of what unity is and why it matters.

At a time when we are so excited about our own identity, and our ideas of community are compromised by efforts to belong to a global village, it is the job of our priests to remind us that what is most interesting about us is what we might be together. It is this truth that Clement and Michael Ramsey, in very different ways, understood and explained, and both of them made the clergy instruments of the gospel of a common salvation.

Notes

1 Ephesians 1.22; Colossians 1.18; 1 Peter 2.9; Matthew 21.33; 1 Corinthians 3.9; Revelation 21.2; Ephesians 5.25.
2 1 Corinthians 12.4–10; Romans 12.6.
3 R. Williams, *Silence and Honey Cakes: The Wisdom of the Desert*, Oxford: Lion, 2003, p. 95.
4 M. Robinson, *Gilead*, London: Virago, 2004, pp. 152–3.
5 Ephesians 4.13.
6 Clement of Rome, *First Epistle*, 1, ANF, 1.
7 Clement of Rome, *First Epistle*, 47.
8 Clement of Rome, *First Epistle*, 40
9 Clement of Rome, *First Epistle*, 41.
10 Clement of Rome, *First Epistle*, 20
11 Clement of Rome, *First Epistle*, 42.
12 *Didache*, 15, trans. A. Roberts and J. Donaldson, http://www.earlychristianwritings.com/text/didache-roberts.html.
13 See above, p. 67. Other Anglicans have relied on Clement and fought this corner, notably R. C. Moberly: 'That ministerial office depends upon orderly transmission from those empowered to transmit the authority to ordain, that is upon a real apostolic succession, is maintained by St Clement as strongly as it is possible for a man to maintain it.' R. C. Moberly, *Ministerial Priesthood*, London: John Murray, 1899, pp. 116, 114. The Roman Catholic Church also cites Clement. It is Clement's authority that is used to establish that men (and only men)

are called to apostolic ministry by the Lord himself: *Catechism of the Catholic Church*, London: Continuum, 1994, 1577.

14 Clement of Rome, *First Epistle*, 42 and n.10.

15 Numbers 26.10.

16 Clement of Rome, *First Epistle*, 3.

17 Clement of Rome, *First Epistle*, 41.

18 Clement of Rome, *First Epistle*, 39.

19 Clement of Rome, *First Epistle*, 37.

20 C. Williams, 'Apologue on the Parable of the Wedding Garment', in *The Image of the City and other Essays* (1958), Eugene, OR: Wipf & Stock 2016, p. 167, quoted in J. V. Taylor, *The Christlike God*, London: SCM Press, 2004, p. 244.

21 Clement of Rome, *First Epistle*, 20.

22 Psalm 148.7–12.

23 Ephesians 4.11–13.

24 *Church Times*, 9 June 1961.

25 It was republished, in a slightly altered form, in 1956.

26 M. Ramsey, *The Gospel and the Catholic Church*, Peabody MA: Hendrickson Publishing, 2009, p. 4.

27 1 John 3.2.

28 Ramsey, *The Gospel and the Catholic Church*, p. 7.

29 Ephesians 5.25; Colossians 1.21–22.

30 1 Corinthians 11.26.

31 1 Corinthians 1.17; 2.2.

32 Ramsey, *The Gospel and the Catholic Church*, p. 27.

33 Ramsey, *The Gospel and the Catholic Church*, p. 27.

34 Ramsey, *The Gospel and the Catholic Church*, p. 36.

35 Ramsey, *The Gospel and the Catholic Church*, p. 50.

36 M. Ramsey, *The Christian Priest Today*, Eugene, OR: Wipf & Stock, 2011, p. 111.

37 Ramsey, *The Gospel and the Catholic Church*, p. 72.

38 M. Ramsey, *The Christian Priest Today*, London: SPCK, 1972, p. 33. All subsequent references to this work are to this edition.

39 Ramsey, *The Christian Priest Today*, p. 14.

40 Ramsey, *The Christian Priest Today*, p. 33.

41 Ramsey, *The Christian Priest Today*, p. 89.

42 Ramsey, *The Christian Priest Today*, p. 89.

43 Ramsey, *The Christian Priest Today*, p. 93; see also p. 78.

44 Ramsey, *The Christian Priest Today*, p. 78.

45 R. Williams, Lecture on the 150th anniversary of Ripon College, Cuddesdon, http://rowanwilliams.archbishopofcanterbury.org/articles.php/2097/the-christian-priest-today-lecture-on-the-occasion-of-the-150th-anniversary-of-ripon-college-cuddesd#sthash.mT4qJTKy.dpuf

46 Williams, Lecture on the 150th anniversary of Ripon College, Cuddesdon.

9

Keeping Your Balance

Ambrose: passionate moderation

In the Norfolk village of Cawston an extraordinary rood screen survives; a company of saints ablaze in red and gold. Before the Reformation, the faithful knelt here and said their prayers surrounded by apostles, the virgin martyrs and famous local saints. To get to the altar, they would have had to walk through the doors of the screen also painted with images: Gregory, Jerome, Augustine and Ambrose, the four Latin Doctors of the Church. So, week by week, the people of Cawston passed through the teaching of the Church to come into the presence of God made flesh.

Two of these Latin Doctors, Ambrose, Bishop of Milan, and Pope Gregory, wrote about ministry. Ambrose's book *On the Duties of the Clergy* (*De officiis Ministrorum*) is the older of the two. It is a significant work not just because Ambrose was a theologian of powerful intellect, but because it had to rise to a very specific challenge. Living at the end of the fourth century, Ambrose belonged to the generation that escaped persecution only to face the subtler temptations of a Church apparently at ease with the world. Christianity was now the religion of emperors, and when Ambrose encountered the powers of this world he was more often accuser than accused. Towards the end of his life he forced the Emperor, Theodosius, to repent publicly after a massacre in Thessalonica. He defied the Arian Empress, Justina, stared down her soldiers and berated her from the pulpit. That volatile political history, the clash of culture and the degree of risk that went with it, is the necessary background to reading Ambrose's three books *On the Duties of the Clergy.*

On the Duties of the Clergy appears to have been written for the priests of Ambrose's Diocese of Milan. Like Gregory of Nazianzus, Ambrose had been ordained suddenly and he felt ill equipped: 'For I was carried off from the judgment seat, and the garb of office, to enter on the priesthood, and began to teach you, what I myself had not yet learnt.'[1] Ambrose set out to teach the clergy what he felt he had needed to know. He was to some extent talking to himself, and from the beginning he was worried about words and carelessness: 'How many have I seen to fall into sin by speaking, but scarcely one by keeping silent.'[2] His argument is littered with scriptural references, but the assumptions he made would have been familiar to pagan Romans too. In Greek and Roman culture words were a form of temptation. The desire to speak for effect, the desire to say words that might get a reaction, or wound, was understood to be strong and deadly:

> Bind up thy words that they run not riot, and grow wanton, and gather up sins for themselves in too much talking. Let them be rather confined, and held back within their own banks. An overflowing river quickly gathers mud.[3]

Ambrose noted words are like water, they can flow and flood:

> let there be a yoke and a balance to thy words, that is, humility and moderation, that thy tongue may be subject to thy mind. Let it be held in check with a tight rein; let it have its own means of restraint, whereby it can be recalled to moderation.[4]

Ambrose wrote and thought in a particular way. His training had taught him to define things and to make distinctions, to separate one from another. He makes careful distinctions between different kinds of duty, dividing the useful from the virtuous and the ordinary from the perfect. His own ministry was passionate and controversial, but he was a true Roman and that meant that he regarded moderation, balance and proportion as the great virtues. He favoured 'measured speech', mercy and modesty of dress and manner.[5] He even argued that the clergy should not walk fast.[6] Ambrose expected the clergy to lead a life of heroic, but quiet, virtue: 'We ought to be humble, gentle, mild, serious, patient. We must keep the mean in all things, so that a calm countenance and quiet speech may show that there is no vice in our lives.'[7]

This love of moderation informed his faith. He much admired the publican of the parable who prayed quietly. He urged his readers to avoid the theatres, banquets and parties of temptation. He thought the clergy did best if they simply stayed away from the places where trouble might lie, rather than fight all their battles in public. Suspicious of a hearty ministry, Ambrose can sound over-cautious, or even insipid. He was neither. He did not write about moderation because he was introverted, or because it came naturally. He found this disciplined virtue hard; he called it a 'battle'. Duty mattered to him because that is how the life of faith is lived now. Mere duty was but the means to the end; in Ambrose's mind, it paved a way to heaven.

Ambrose was quick to point out that both the Roman, Cicero, and the Athenian, Panaetius, had things to say about moderation and duty. He knew he was not beginning with a distinctively Christian insight. Urging the clergy to grind out the truth and keep crazy instinct in check, he could sound as though he was offering conventional and rather austere Roman morality:

> by its very nature reflection diffuses tranquillity and calm; and passion sends forth the impulse to act. Let us then be ready to allow reflection on good things to enter into our mind, and to make passion submit to reason.[8]

Beneath and behind these old ideas, however, another theme was running. Ambrose, first a politician and then a bishop who knew his way around the palaces of emperors, never lived so much in this world that he ceased to imagine the courts of heaven. Ambrose was always focused on what lay ahead. This kind of advice can feel a bit unwelcome. When we talk about ministry, we talk about 'getting alongside' and 'joining in'. The language we have developed for ministry is shaped now by Myers Briggs, the Enneagram and Belbin. It is not 'duty' we talk about, but personality. When Harry Williams looked back across his ministry he called his book *Becoming What I Am*, as he charted a painful journey to self-acceptance. His was a very particular inner turmoil, but it is an increasingly popular view of how a vocation to ministry is to be understood and worked out. So, for example, Andrew Clitherow can write about 'being reminded of the need to be ourselves'.[9] Duty and restraint then quickly begin to look like a straitjacket, cramping what is best about us. In a changing culture, the clergy have to adapt and find a different language to frame the words of hope. Increasingly, priests need to know their own emotional range and be ready to express it (without falling into the trap of simply talking about themselves). Our own feelings become a resource for ministry. No surprise, then, that in a recent excellent book about ministry John Pritchard writes: 'The core of a valued ministry is a network of valued relationships. A priest has to establish his or her human credibility before anything else.'[10] Nothing here about 'duty'. So what sense can we make of Ambrose?

First, we must avoid the mistake of assuming all this talk of duty was a summons away from the world. Ambrose's own ministry, with its dramatic confrontations and swashbuckling sermons, was a ministry of passionate engagement. Once, and not so long ago, Christians had seemed like aliens, struggling to explain how they fitted into society; now, suddenly, they had become the establishment and they were left wondering in what ways they were at all distinctive. That was the challenge for Ambrose: how to live in the world and not be of the world. The answer he fashioned was that the Christians lived in the world, but with virtue; their distinctive characteristic was godliness. Ambrose was not calling priests away from the world. He was asking them to behave distinctively, but still in a way that society could understand and appreciate. Second, Ambrose wanted the clergy to be distinctive, but not peculiar.

He asked them to display a virtue others would admire. He did not want them to be peculiar, but he did want them all to be, in some sense, the *same*. It was the *same* duty that would mark them out, the *same* moderation, prudence and fortitude that they would all share. Ambrose, remember, had an eye on what lay ahead, the heavenly city, the community to which we will belong for ever. Writing about priesthood, he was also writing about ways in which we can live together. Like priests in scripture, he argued, the clergy see things differently and do things differently because they have seen the Kingdom.

> First, thou shalt see the deep things of God, which needs wisdom. Next, thou must keep watch for the people; this requires justice. Thou must defend the camp and guard the tabernacle, which needs fortitude. Thou must show thyself continent and sober, and this needs temperance.[11]

That is why the clergy need to conform to some shared duty, some common identity and common purpose, because the future has got hold of them and will not let them go. They have a common identity and pressing concerns.

> Entangle not thyself in the affairs of this life, for thou art fighting for God. For if he who fights for the emperor is forbidden by human laws to enter upon lawsuits, to do any legal business, or to sell merchandise; how much more ought he who enters upon the warfare of faith to keep from every kind of business.[12]

It is precisely because the clergy pursue a life of blessedness and have their eyes and minds fixed on divine things that they then become part of the local community. Their virtues are virtues that bind the community together: wisdom, judgement and, above all, love.[13] The virtue of the clergy, then, is attractive, not dour, social, not aloof.

> Let there be peace among you, which passeth all understanding. Love one another. Nothing is sweeter than charity,

nothing more blessed than peace. Ye yourselves know that I
have ever loved you and do now love you above all others. As
the children of one father ye have become united under the
bond of brotherly affection.[14]

When the faithful walked through the gates of the rood screen
in Cawston, on their way to make their communion, they
passed St Ambrose. They passed through the teaching of the
Church as they drew closer to Christ. It is precisely what *On
the Duties of the Clergy* assumes. In celebrating what scripture
teaches, in sitting under the teaching of the Church and in
adopting a common discipline and a passionate moderation,
there is an invitation to community that cannot be worked out
in any other way. Only those who accept a little restraint, only
those who resign the great project of self-improvement can ever
forget themselves enough to become one in Christ. Ambrose
reminds us that, strangely, it is duty and conformity that will
set us free.

Gregory the Great, ministry in the midst

'A lawyer stood up to test Jesus. "Teacher," he said, "what
must I do to inherit eternal life?"'[15] The lawyer wanted definition. Told to love his neighbour, he asked about the small
print. He was told the parable of the good Samaritan, and
that ends with a question. The gospel is salvation and God is
a God of mission, but there is no system and no process that
will make it tidy. Jesus asked us to follow him, he urged us to
'repent and believe', he answered one question with another,
his disciples lived in trust, not certainty. The way of Christ is
not the simple business of doing one thing well. Ministry, by
the same token, is not a particular task, or the application of
a particular principle, as if there might be just one thing that
needs doing. Despite all those books that suggest there is one
method, three steps, or just five habits, ministry is a way of life
that is rich and various. That is why the *Common Worship*
ordination service is more suggestive than instructive.

They are to be messengers, watchmen and stewards of the Lord; they are to teach and to admonish, to feed and provide for his family, to search for his children in the wilderness of this world's temptations, and to guide them through its confusions, that they may be saved through Christ for ever. Formed by the word, they are to call their hearers to repentance and to declare in Christ's name the absolution and forgiveness of their sins.[16]

The poet Gerard Manley Hopkins used to worry that if he took too much delight in the sheer abundance and diversity of creation he would lose sight of the Creator. He came slowly to the realization that it was not his job to tidy up all that abundance, but to celebrate the fact that it is held together in God. We do not, must not, keep it simple. In the early 1970s Annie Dillard spent a year living at Tinker Creek in the Blue Ridge Mountains. She was gripped by the extravagant abundance of life all around her. Taking delight in what felt like bubbling confusion, she recoiled from order and routine. With a kind of horror she described the work of the scientist Fabre, who tricked pine processionary caterpillars into moving aimlessly round the rim of a vase, following an endless circular thread.

I want out of this still air. What street-corner vendor wound the key on the backs of the tin soldiers and abandoned them to the sidewalk and crashings over the curb? Elijah mocked the prophets of Baal, who lay a bullock on a woodpile and begged Baal to consume it ... The prophets of Baal gashed themselves with knives and lancets and the wood stayed wood. The fixed is the world without fire – dead flint, dead tinder; and nowhere a spark. It is motion without direction, force without power, the aimless procession of caterpillars round the rim of a vase, and I hate it because at any moment I myself might step to that charmed and glistening thread.[17]

The variety matters. When the former Bishop of Oxford wrote a book on ministry and tried to divide up the task he found he had 16 different headings. So he offered us an impressive and slightly alarming list of things that need doing; a list that will have even the bravest and best of us feeling the need for a lie down. Yet he still had to admit 'there is no secret out there waiting our discovery'.[18]

It is this truth we must grasp if we are going to make sense of the life and work of Gregory the Great. He lived a life very nearly swamped by the scale and variety of what lay before him. He steeled himself to the demands of a constantly shifting focus. For Gregory, ministry always had to be *this* and *that*. He would have preferred something very different; Gregory longed for a life of disciplined seclusion. Instead he was made Bishop of Rome in 590, just as the Roman imperial achievement finally collapsed.[19] The Lombards invaded Italy in 568 and eight years later annihilated the imperial army. There were a few good years, but 589 was spectacularly bad. The Tiber flooded and destroyed the papal granaries. Plague followed and carried off Pope Pelagius. Gregory's inheritance was bleak: 'We see in this city the walls going to ruin, the houses falling down, the churches destroyed by the whirlwind and the buildings crumbling from old age, because ruin collapses upon ruin.'[20] He was convinced that he was living in the last times.

> Cities are overthrown, camps uprooted, churches destroyed; and no tiller of the ground inhabits our land ... In the passing away, then, of all things, we ought to take thought how that all that we have loved was nothing. View, therefore, with anxious heart the approaching day of the eternal judge, and by repenting anticipate its terrors.[21]

In the midst of all this decay Gregory called on an immense intellectual discipline which could impose order on near chaotic circumstance. He produced one of the most influential of all the books written for the clergy, *The Book of Pastoral Rule*. That sustained desire for order determined his approach and the shape of the book: 'This book is divided into four separate heads of argument, that it may approach the reader's mind by allegations arranged in order – by certain steps.' Even so there is no attempt to disguise, or tidy away, the complexity of the task:

we must especially consider after what manner every one should come to supreme rule; and, duly arriving at it, after what manner he should live; and, living well, after what manner he should teach; and, teaching aright, with how great consideration every day he should become aware of his own infirmity; lest either humility fly from the approach, or life be at variance with the arrival, or teaching be wanting to the life, or presumption unduly exalt the teaching.[22]

In truth, although priests have read it with profit, *The Book of Pastoral Rule* is intended as a guide for bishops. It is a particular book, written for a particular time. The conventions and assumptions of the earlier Church were fading. Bishops were beginning to look more and more like imperial officials and it was inevitably assumed that they would have the same competence as those officials. Where once a man might be seized and suddenly ordained (like Gregory of Nazianzus or Ambrose), now the Church looked not just for personality and learning, but also for training and experience. So, in Gregory we find for the first time a more detailed reflection on formation for ministry. He thought that medical practitioners had learnt a proper seriousness, but the clergy had not. He was scandalized by those who rushed in where angels feared to tread: 'How often do men who have no knowledge whatever of spiritual precepts fearlessly profess themselves physicians of the heart, though those who are ignorant of the effect of drugs blush to appear as physicians of the flesh.'[23]

Then, like so many writers before and since, Gregory insisted that holiness matters. It is not enough to learn ministry, you must live it. Fail to do that, and you become a shepherd who leads sheep to water and then kicks up mud into the water they must drink:

And verily the sheep drink the water fouled by their feet, when any of those subject to them follow not the words which they hear, but only imitate the bad examples which they see ... no one does more harm in the Church than one who has the name and rank of sanctity, while he acts perversely.[24]

The seriousness of the task made Gregory impatient with those who pushed themselves forward and those who hung back. It might feel like humility to refuse preferment, but sometimes it is not. Gregory understood the doubts and the bursts of self-confidence that unsettle our work. He knew that the skills and gifts we think we have can suddenly seem inadequate when they are tested by big responsibilities. The pastoral gifts, the compassion and sensitivity, we first developed do not necessarily equip us to care for cities, counties or councils divided by faction and ill will:

> it is generally the case that the very practice of good deeds which was maintained in tranquillity is lost in the occupation of government; since even an unskilful person guides a ship along a straight course in a calm sea; but in one disturbed by the waves of tempest even the skilled sailor is confounded.[25]

Ministry is a commitment to begin something that we cannot control, or determine, and that will expose both our strengths and our weaknesses. Confident in our belief that God gives us gifts and wills us to flourish, we can be seduced into thinking that vocation is just a sustained endorsement of our personality. The real challenge, however, is not how you will deploy your gifts, but how you will contend with your weaknesses. Gregory was not at all sure that his vocation lay in *public* ministry; he believed he was supposed to be a monk. *The Book of Pastoral Rule* is his attempt to convince himself that it is not simply a question of being directed by your sense of your own giftedness.[26] He reminds us that a vocation is not ultimately measured by what we are; it is a test of what we might become.

He set out the challenge and then considered what kind of person might suffice. He described a person who has mastered the lurching demands of emotion and desire; one who is not driven by the need for praise, success or status. Then he explored the theme of moderation that so interested Ambrose, and lifted that discussion to a new level. What Gregory looked for in a minister was one who could build a community generous in its variety; one who could manage the boundaries between mercy and justice, between decency and disapproval:

> who through the bowels of compassion is quickly moved to pardon, yet is never bent down from the fortress of rectitude by pardoning more than is meet; who perpetrates no unlawful deeds, yet deplores those perpetrated by others as though they were his own; who out of affection of heart sympathizes with another's infirmity, and so rejoices in the good of his neighbour as though it were his own advantage.[27]

This ability to sustain a life that never lurches into excess of any kind is a dominant theme of *The Book of Pastoral Rule*. In Gregory there was never *one* thing you should do, the task is never defined by a single outcome; it is always this *and* that, always resisting the temptation to be too particular. Bishops should manage the boundaries between speech and silence, and be concerned for inward and outward. Similarly, Gregory was clear that no one should be a bishop unless their eyes are lifted to heaven, yet they must not be tempted to settle there. Like the angels Jacob saw, preachers must know how to ascend and how to descend.[28] He warned of the temptations of swift action. He knew about the temptation of all that busy, tiring work that people notice and applaud, which then prevents us from doing the work people do not see, like saying our prayers.[29] He also warned of the subtle temptations of passionate commitment. Righteous anger, he suggested, can be impressive, but it can also be intoxicating, and what feels like virtue rapidly turns into vice: 'inordinate laxity is believed to be loving-kindness, and unbridled wrath is accounted the virtue of spiritual zeal. Often precipitate action is taken for the efficacy of promptness, and tardiness for the deliberation of seriousness.'[30] Even virtue can begin to admire itself and turn into vanity.

Gregory was well aware that he was setting out a demanding agenda. He believed church office (he called it 'government' or 'rule' because it was chiefly responsibility for others) was full of confusions. His own experience suggested to him that the mind was always pulled in different directions. There was a further challenge too, and it was one that came to dominate the latter part of *The Book of Pastoral Rule*. Not only must a minister manage all the complex boundaries of personal emotion. A pastor also has to know that people are different and our relationships with them must be different. He produced a long list of distinctions, a catalogue of different responsibilities. Here is just a taste:

Men and women.
The poor and the rich.
The joyful and the sad.
The too silent, and those who spend time in much speaking.
The obstinate and the fickle.
The gluttonous and the abstinent.
Those who, though able to preach worthily, are afraid through excessive humility; and those whom imperfection or age debars from preaching, and yet rashness impels to it.
Those who have had experience of carnal intercourse, and those who are ignorant of it.
Those who bewail misdeeds, yet forsake them not; and those who forsake them, yet bewail them not.
Those who even praise the unlawful things they do; and those who censure what is wrong, yet avoid it not.[31]

The idea that we must minister differently to different people had already been explored. Gregory, though, subjected it to a penetrating analysis and explored human psychology in the process. He was determined to allow variety and yet never sacrifice the unity of the Church and faith.[32] He was strong too on the temptations of office:

commonly a ruler, from the very fact of his being pre-eminent over others, is puffed up ... surrounded by unbounded favour, he loses his inward sense of truth; and, forgetful of himself, he scatters himself on the voices of other men, and believes himself to be such as outwardly he hears himself called rather than such as he ought inwardly to have judged himself to be.[33]

Gregory knew it is perfectly possible to act the priest, without ever really *being* the priest. It is tempting to let people put you on the pedestal they have reserved for the vicar and there are days when it seems a lot more comfortable for you, and for them, if you stay there. 'You must be very busy,' people say, and you smile bravely and fix your eyes on the distance, then everyone begins to feel faintly noble without ever wondering why a role has suddenly swept away relationships. In a vocation in which there is such a need to stand apart, climb pulpit steps, chair meetings, and in which there is so much ritual, all those sermons and services, it is a constant struggle not to turn ministry into performance.

The Book of Pastoral Rule is a searing account of the inner life of the clergy. It is a fundamental assumption of the book that the work of a priest imposes a particular discipline and character on those who are called into ministry. So, for example, Gregory insists that a priest must be 'always chief in action'. What he means is that priests should not think that the important work is done in private, in counselling and caring for individuals, but accept that this is a public office in which they must expect to lead by example. We need to be clear that Gregory never thought that priesthood was the highest, or only, calling; he simply pointed out that it was a public and visible vocation. The test of ministry in Gregory's eyes was not the influence you might have with individuals, but how you turned those individuals into community.

Again and again he identified the danger that you could lose your balance, give too much priority or too little. He knew that there was a need to draw close to people in sympathy and understanding and a need to draw apart in prayer, and that both movements are necessary.[34] A clergy caught up in that ceaseless movement of angels ascending and descending would learn a love of balance. He saw no need to stand always apart, vigilant and aloof in case it was necessary suddenly to speak out. Instead, he wanted the clergy to be good companions and equals to those who live out the faith. He wanted them to speak against sin where they saw it without behaving as though they were always suspicious, or always morally superior. He had no time for the one who strives so hard for dignity and rectitude that, 'being a man, he disdains to be like unto men'.[35]

The life he described is demanding and its hallmark is the constant exercise in balance. He described a constant process of discernment and a ceaseless vigilance. He pleaded for a ministry that was fundamentally human. The clergy are not called to be holy so that they can be impressive or save themselves, they are called to be holy so that we can all learn holiness together.

> [L]et him consider the admonition of the Psalmist, *Praise him with timbrel and chorus*. For in the timbrel a dry and beaten skin resounds, but in the chorus voices are associated in concord. Whosoever then afflicts his body, but forsakes concord, praises GOD indeed with timbrel, but praises Him not with chorus.[36]

His book was never a counsel of perfection. He lived with a fear of failure, 'lest in helping others he desert himself, lest in lifting up others he fall'.[37] He did not rely on hard work, nor on deep learning to sustain the ministry; he depended rather on the community of which he knew he was a part. He may have written about 'rule', but he always understood his place within the Church to be as simply one more sinner utterly dependent on grace:

> being intent on shewing what a Pastor ought to be, I have been as an ill-favoured painter portraying a handsome man; and how I direct others to the shore of perfection, while myself still tossed among the waves of transgressions. But in the shipwreck of this present life sustain me, I beseech thee, by the plank of thy prayer, that, since my own weight sinks me down, the hand of thy merit may raise me up.[38]

Chief pastor in the community of prayer, Gregory was not too proud to ask for the prayers of others, nor was he seduced in difficult times by the lure of simple solutions and blind conviction. His *Book of Pastoral Rule* is a call to a ministry that must never turn into a race to be run (and won); it is instead just an act of balance.

J. B. Lightfoot

The late nineteenth century was the age of the theological college. New foundations sprang up, chiefly in cathedral cities where, by all accounts, curmudgeonly canons sneered at the new learning.[39] Bishops cared about ministerial training. At Cuddesdon, Samuel Wilberforce, the Bishop of Oxford, extended that concern into a running battle with the staff and students over churchmanship. In Durham, J. B. Lightfoot (Bishop 1879–89) was less abrasive, but learning and ministry mattered just as much. He was still urging Cambridge friends, 'Send me up men to the North,' as he was dying.[40] Durham was an established university city, but the new bishop took the training of ordinands into his own hands and his own home. It was an intense and particular experience:

> He is accessible to their difficulties and their doubts, if they have any; but, a thing more remarkable, he is open to all their kittenhood of mirth and fun. To hear him alone with them is to feel you are on the edge of a circle, which tempts you almost to stand on tiptoe and look over and wish you were inside.[41]

Lightfoot was a formidable scholar with a huge sense of vocation and moral purpose. Training ordinands was an intense business for him. By the time he came to ordain the men he had taught, and who had shared his home, his natural rhetoric was fuelled with feeling.

> One sunset and one sunrise more. Then the irrevocable step is taken. The stream is crossed. The frontier line is traversed. The door is closed upon the past. You have all doubtless thought seriously over the momentous nature of the change. I should do you a cruel wrong, if I supposed that you – any one of you – could face this crisis lightly or carelessly. It will be to you an occasion of anxious misgiving, of deep self-abasement, of silent heart-searching, of awe and trembling; and yet withal of profound, over-flowing thankfulness.[42]

At this point we need to put Lightfoot in context. The language he used was his own and his emotion was real. He was addressing a public crisis in the Church. Ministry was changing because the place of the Church in society was changing. One set of associations that had depended on patronage and tithe in a culture that had allowed some clergy to live easily and relatively indolent, while others worked hard for mere crumbs, was replaced with something very different. Prosperous country clergy ceased to identify themselves so readily with hunting squires, and poor parsons emerged from penury and subservience. At the same time, priests no longer filled the roles they had long occupied as justices of the peace, administrators of the poor law, or health visitors. Instead, they began to work harder at pastoral work, leading worship, renovating church buildings and teaching the faith. This was a new identity with new social standing; status and respect were differently earned. The clergy began to get to associate in deaneries and to meet in clerical societies. They started to read clerical newspapers like *The Ecclesiastical Gazette* or *The Clerical Journal*, they looked one another up in *The Clerical Directory*, first published in 1841, and they studied the handbooks on ministry that were now produced in startling numbers. The clergy acquired an identity that set them apart and, significantly, they began to wear a kind of uniform.[43] This was the world in which Lightfoot trained his ordinands. This was why he set out to give them an identity that would set them apart. It is for this reason that Lightfoot's ordination charges spoke with a new and heady stress on 'great change, new work, new life' and 'a past beyond recall'.

Sitting in a chapel in Ely, with my own ordination looming, just 'one sunset and one sunrise more', I was nearly carried away by the conviction that I wasn't up to the task. Lightfoot tackled that dread head on.

You are on the threshold of a new career, on the eve of a new life, a new career, a new life, fraught with issues of infinite moment to yourselves, not only to yourselves (that is only a small thing), but (it may be) to hundreds and thousands of others besides, a new career, a new life, full of hope, full of fear, charged with a tremendous alternative of good or of evil.[44]

There was no doubt in Lightfoot's mind that ordination changes things. He spoke of 'a new life' and believed that ordained ministers had to acquire a personality that matched the promises they made. Knowing that facing that challenge the clergy can become obsessively introspective, he suggested the solution was self-forgetfulness and steady routine. The task ahead was clear and there was plenty of work to be getting on with: 'Here is a definite thing to be done, and you will do it.' Hard work would help steady the nerves, but Lightfoot knew he had overworked and he did not labour that point. More importantly (and in a way familiar from so many books about ministry), Lightfoot urged ordinands to remember, 'It is not your doing but God's doing': 'let this be your one vow, your one prayer, "God helping me, I will do His work, because it is His work. God helping me, I will preach His truth, because it is His truth".'[45] Ministry can feel like a roller coaster, and he wanted his ordinands to find a more a settled experience: 'I will not be discouraged by failure; I will not be elated by success. The success and the failure are not my concern, but His.'[46]

He talked about the way the work takes over, about clergy who develop an interest in 'results', and about the optimism, or pessimism, that can breed:

[P]ut away, relentlessly away, all thought of the results. You cannot control them. The operations are in your hands; the issues are far beyond your reach. And, if you cannot control them, so neither can you estimate them. You see only a little way; but God's purposes are far.

He told the ordinands that nothing can be more false than human estimates of success and failure and reminded them that their model was Christ who 'failed in every purpose of his heart'.[47]

Some of his ordination addresses set out to describe the character of ministry in greater detail. For all the rhetoric, Lightfoot had an intensely practical desire to see the work of the Church getting done. Like other writers and preachers before him, he spoke of the importance of clergy living up to the standard they set for others.[48] Lightfoot, though, had more to say. He talked about steering a course between imposing yourself on every situation and never imposing yourself at all.

> Remember that you are ambassadors, but remember also that you are slaves. Do not merge the ambassador in the slave, and do not lose the slave in the ambassador. If you forget that you are ambassadors, your work will be feeble, flaccid, listless and inefficient, because nerveless and sinewless. If you forget that you are slaves, it will be arrogant and harsh and repulsive; it will win no sympathy, because it will show no sympathy; it will gain no adherents, because it will make no sacrifices.[49]

Lightfoot understood that it is not enough to know the truth; you have to think how you will help others to hear it. Ministry demands self-restraint:

> with you nothing is unimportant, nothing is trifling. There is the fault of temper, the impatience of opposition, the stiffness of self-assertion, a magnifying of self which veils itself from itself under the guise of magnifying of your office. It is not in vain that at the outset of your ministry the prayer is offered for you that you may be modest and humble.[50]

A priest who cannot apologize, a priest who cannot accept criticism, a priest who cannot bear patiently with someone else's pomposity, or foolishness, might have virtue of a kind. He or she might even be more sinned against than sinning, but he or she will also be a solitary, dour figure on the outside of any community looking in.

Lightfoot took ordained ministry seriously, but he was never a champion of clericalism. He knew that vocation may be an individual calling, but it can only be worked out in community. He could write passionately about the way Christ calls an individual: 'Has He spoken to you? Has He entreated you? Has He commanded you? This voice of His, how is it heard? This will of His, how is it expressed?'[51] Still, though, he would insist that this calling made you into someone living in relation to others. He told ordinands that love was a characteristic of true ministry and then reminded them that love was a gift of God.[52] Nothing terribly surprising in that, but Lightfoot pressed the conclusion home. Love is the heart of ministry and love is a quality found in lay people as well as in the ordained. Ordinands were told that their ministry was shared with others.

> What is your diaconate but an intensification of the function of ministering which is incumbent on all believers alike? What is your priesthood but a concentration of the priesthood of the whole people of Christ? Yes, you will do well to press upon your people in season and out of season that the Church of Christ is one great priesthood, one vast spiritual brotherhood, gathered together of all sorts and conditions of men, for the good of humanity.[53]

The theological foundations of this passage had been worked out years before and published as an essay on *The Christian Ministry*, in Lightfoot's commentary on Philippians. There, his profound sense that Christian faith calls us into community finds expression in a description of the Kingdom that is to come, an equal and inclusive society in which there is no 'sacerdotal system'.

> It interposes no sacrificial tribe or class between God and man, by whose intervention alone God is reconciled and man forgiven. Each individual member holds personal communion with the Divine Head. To Him immediately he is responsible, and from Him directly he obtains pardon and draws strength.[54]

Lightfoot believed that 'all Christians are priests alike'.[55] Indeed, he always found the term 'priesthood' uncomfortable, preferring 'the silence of the Apostolic writers'.[56] In this theology, an ordained priesthood only becomes necessary because the Church needs order: 'the minister's function is *representative* without being *vicarial*. He is a priest, as the mouthpiece, the delegate of a priestly race. His acts are not his own, but the acts of the congregation.'[57]

Nothing is unimportant

The Roman virtues of Ambrose and Gregory and the Victorian seriousness of Lightfoot are unfamiliar territory now. The stress that falls on character, duty and fitting yourself to the work is not the way we usually think of ministry today. We have learnt to be wary of overwork and self-sacrifice and we celebrate different virtues. All three authors share a realism about the daunting demands of ministry and remind us that resilience might be one of the qualities we need. That is worth hearing. Significant as that insight is, however, their real contribution to our understanding of ministry probably lies elsewhere. Under pressure because there are simply fewer clergy than there were, under pressure because so many of us are facing pastoral reorganization and falling electoral rolls, under pressure because the context of ministry is changing and our grip on culture is much weaker, priests have to think harder than they did about how they might make an impact. Impact comes with focus, and one of the characteristics of ministry now is that we are increasingly specific about what we expect. We advertise for people who will deliver growth, for leaders, and for specified skills. That is a necessary discipline as we strive to appoint the right people to the right posts. The difficulty is that we may be beginning to think that ministry is *only* about leadership and growth.

Moderation, duty and Lightfoot's alarming suggestion that we are 'slaves' are all reminders that ministry expects more from us than we can define or determine. There is more than one subject in the curriculum, more than one way of being a priest. In Ambrose and Gregory we encounter a significant and now timely challenge to remember that ministry is not a specialism. In a church committed to straplines and mission statements these are bishops who ask us to consider the possibility that the gospel might be more than that – more profound, more glorious and much more demanding.

Notes

1 Ambrose, *On the Duties of the Clergy*, 1.1.4, trans. H. de Romestin, *N&PNF 2S*, 12.

2 Ambrose, *On the Duties of the Clergy*, 1.2.5

3 Ambrose, *On the Duties of the Clergy*, 1.3.12.

4 Ambrose, *On the Duties of the Clergy*, 1.4.13

5 Ambrose, *On the Duties of the Clergy*, 1.10.35; 11.38; 18.67.

6 Ambrose, *On the Duties of the Clergy*, 1.18.74.

7 Ambrose, *On the Duties of the Clergy*, 1.20.89.

8 Ambrose, *On the Duties of the Clergy*, 1.22.98; 21.90.

9 A. Clitherow, *Renewing Faith in Ordained Ministry*, London: SPCK, 2004, p. 102.

10 J. Pritchard, *The Life and Work of a Priest*, London: SPCK, 2007, pp. 69–70.

11 Ambrose, *On the Duties of the Clergy*, 1.50.260.

12 Ambrose, *On the Duties of the Clergy*, 36.185

13 Ambrose, *On the Duties of the Clergy*, 2.8.40.

14 Ambrose, *On the Duties of the Clergy*, 30.155

15 Luke 10.25ff.

16 *Common Worship: Ordination Services*, London: Church House Publishing, 2007.

17 Annie Dillard, *Pilgrim at Tinker Creek* in *Three by Annie Dillard: Pilgrim at Tinker Creek, An American Childhood, The Writing Life*, New York: Harper Perennial, 1990, pp. 69–70.

18 See Pritchard, *The Life and Work of a Priest*, p. 159.

19 R. A. Markus, *Gregory the Great*, Cambridge: Cambridge University Press, 1997, pp. 3ff.

20 Gregory, *Homily in Ezekiel* 2.6.22, quoted in W. H. C. Frend, *The Rise of Christianity*, London: Darton, Longman & Todd, 1986, p. 885.

21 Gregory, *Epistles*, 3.29, 'To the Presbyters and Clergy of Mediolanum', trans. J. Barmby, *N&PNF 2S*, 12.

22 Gregory, *The Book of Pastoral Rule*, 1.1, trans. J. Barmby, *N&PNF 2S*, 12.

23 Gregory, *Pastoral Rule*, 1.1.

24 Gregory, *Pastoral Rule*, 1.2.

25 Gregory, *Pastoral Rule*, 1.9.

26 Markus, *Gregory the Great*, p. 14.

27 Gregory, *Pastoral Rule*, 1.10.

28 Gregory, *Pastoral Rule*, 2.5.

29 Gregory, *Pastoral Rule*, 2.7.

30 Gregory, *Pastoral Rule*, 2.9.

31 Gregory, *Pastoral Rule*, 3.1.

32 Markus, *Gregory the Great*, p. 73.

33 Gregory, *Pastoral Rule*, 2.6.

34 Gregory, *Pastoral Rule*, 2.5.

35 Gregory, *Pastoral Rule*, 2.6.

36 Gregory, *Pastoral Rule*, 3.22.

37 Gregory, *Pastoral Rule*, 4.

38 Gregory, *Pastoral Rule*, 4.

39 Owen Chadwick, *The Victorian Church*, London: A. & C. Black 1970, II, p. 382.

40 *Bishop Lightfoot*, from *The Quarterly Review* (1894), p. 66. Available online at http://anglicanhistory.org/lightfoot/westcott1894/.

41 *Bishop Lightfoot*, from *The Quarterly Review*, p. 74.

42 J. B. Lightfoot, *Ordination Addresses* (preached to deacons in 1882, 1885, and 1889), London: Macmillan, 1890, pp. 3, 4.

43 A. Russell, *The Clerical Profession*, London: SPCK, 1980, pp. 28–49.

44 Lightfoot, *Ordination Addresses*, pp. 3, 4 [preached in 1880, 1883 and 1887].

45 Lightfoot, *Ordination Addresses*, p. 6.

46 Lightfoot, *Ordination Addresses*, p. 6.

47 Lightfoot, *Ordination Addresses*, p. 9.

48 Lightfoot, *Ordination Addresses*, p. 24.

49 Lightfoot, *Ordination Addresses*, p. 47.

50 Lightfoot, *Ordination Addresses*, p. 79.

51 Lightfoot, *Ordination Addresses*, p. 37.

52 Lightfoot, *Ordination Addresses*, p. 57.

53 Lightfoot, *Ordination Addresses*, pp. 57, 58.

54 J. B. Lightfoot, 'The Christian Ministry', in *St Paul's Epistle to the Philippians*, London: Macmillan, 1873, p. 179.

55 Lightfoot, 'The Christian Ministry', p. 183.

56 Lightfoot, 'The Christian Ministry', p. 265.

57 Lightfoot, 'The Christian Ministry', p. 266.

10

Spiritual Traffic

Stupor mundi

In 1624, Joseph Hall, the Dean of Worcester, preached to the clergy of the Church of England assembled, at the beginning of Convocation, in St Paul's Cathedral. He took as his text 1 Corinthians 12.4, 'there are diversities of ministries'. For Hall, this was a very good day indeed in a church that was living up to its calling.

> Ye are here met ... Most Reverend Father in God, Reverend Bishops, Venerable Deans, Archdeacons, Brethren of the clergy ... Ye are met in one; and here is unity: ye are many of you met from the utmost parts of this large province; and here is manifold diversity.[1]

This was a Latin sermon so it all sounded very grand indeed. Hall debated gifts and diversity for a few minutes and made the obvious point, that we should use our different gifts for the common good. Beneath the measured beat of his prose, however, there was an unusual and extravagant optimism. Hall was convinced that he was in the best of company and that here, in the convocation arranged before him, there was a very particular kind of diversity and giftedness. Then his enthusiasm rather got the better of him:

> It is a great word, that I shall speak; and yet I must and will say it, without all, either arrogance or flattery; *Stupor mundi Clerus Britannicus*: 'the wonder of the world is the Clergy of Britain'. So many learned divines, so many eloquent preachers shall in vain be sought elsewhere this day.[2]

The idea that anyone might suggest today that the Anglican clergy are the wonder of the world beggars belief. A bit more humility would have been becoming even in the seventeenth century.

The difficulty for Hall, as for everyone who talks or writes about ministry, is that the sheer scale of what we claim can overwhelm us. At the beginning of an ordination service, the bishop reminds us: 'God calls his people to follow Christ, and forms us into a royal priesthood, a holy nation, to declare the wonderful deeds of him who has called us out of darkness into his marvellous light.'[3] We have to use language that is always on the point of running away with us. Chrysostom would have the clergy walk with angels. He was not wrong, of course, it is just not an experience you hear the clergy describe very often. Just 20 years after that extraordinary sermon, Parliament met amid a storm of anti-clericalism and roundly condemned the very bishops, deans and archdeacons that Hall had so admired, and swept away the Church of England altogether. So, it is not just that we struggle with high expectations; we have the added problem that the expectations never stay the same. Time and place will demand one set of priorities, not another. Hall admired learning and preaching. Parliament also valued both, but was particular about the kind of learning and the content of preaching. Ministers soon learn that they will not satisfy the expectations that surround them. They will not even meet the expectations they have for themselves.

Jeremy Taylor, Gilbert Burnet: lives bitter to themselves

Jeremy Taylor, born in Cambridge in 1613 (he was two years older than Richard Baxter), grew up in that angry, edgy church that Hall defended. He was talented and caught the eye of the angular Archbishop of Canterbury, William Laud. His gifts and his prejudices (prejudices that we today call 'High Church') marked him out and, in short order, he was made Chaplain to the King and then Rector of Uppingham. When war broke out, hard decisions had to be made. While Baxter hesitated,

Taylor hurried off to join the royalist army. He was subsequently taken prisoner outside Cardigan castle. His captors delighted in laying hands on this 'most spruce neat formalist, a very ginger-bread Idoll, an Arminian in print'. The rising star now fell rapidly from the heavens. Taylor accepted a chaplaincy from Richard Vaughan, Second Earl of Carbery, at his house at Golden Grove, east of Carmarthen, and lived in near seclusion there, writing books (*The Rule and Exercises of Holy Living*, 1650, and *The Rule and Exercises of Holy Dying*, 1651) that would, one day, make him famous. Retirement, though, did not really suit Taylor. For all his piety and learning he was a restless, even slightly angry, figure and controversy was never far away. He fell out with a Jesuit in print, he fell out with the government (and was imprisoned again as a suspected royalist), and then he fell out with nearly everybody when he cast doubt on the doctrine of original sin. By the time of the Restoration he was in Ireland and in trouble again, but the return of a king to the throne of England saved him. Too difficult and contentious a character to be brought close to home, Taylor was made Bishop of Down and Connor and spent his final years in characteristically acrimonious exchanges with Irish presbyterians.

Taylor wrote about holiness and about ministry. Accustomed to slings and arrows, the title given to the published version of a visitation sermon is deeply suggestive. Where Baxter wrote *The Reformed Pastor*, Taylor chose to issue *Rules and Advices to the Clergy, For their Deportment in their Personal and Publick Capacities*.[4] This was a work about living with difficulty. It opened with conventional advice on setting a good example and advanced arguments made familiar by other authors. He was, though, unusually aware that a Christian minister is a 'publick person' surrounded by temptation. His tone was often more negative than positive. Where others called the clergy to an exemplary holiness, Taylor warned against the dangers of association. He believed the clergy needed to be guarded, defended, cautious. He thought prudence was a characteristic virtue of ministry, but prudence turned out to be just a refusal to conform to the life of the parish.

Let no Minister be governed by the opinion of his People, and destroy his Duty, by unreasonable compliance with their humors ... Be careful so to order your self, that you fall not into temptation and folly in the presence of any of your Charges; and especially that you fall not into chidings and intemperate talkings, and sudden and violent expressions: Never be a party in clamours and scoldings, lest your Calling become useless, and your Person contemptible.[5]

Order and decency were the aim. Taylor told his clergy to use the rites of the Established Church and to insist on her feasts and fasts. Parishes were not to become places of religious experiment and opinion, the minister must discourage speculation and not court popularity. This really was a book of rules, with paragraph after paragraph beginning with the same formula:

Let no Minister be litigious in any thing; not greedy or covetous ...

Let every Minister teach his people the use, practice, methods and benefits of meditation ...

Let every Minister exhort his people to a frequent confession of their sins.[6]

There is something dispiriting about Taylor's grumpy pragmatism (particularly if you have ever savoured the prose in *Holy Living* or *Holy Dying*). His book on ministry has never been held in anything like the affection that some give to George Herbert and others to Richard Baxter. Rules and conformity charm us little, or not at all. It is a book that had its origins in a charge preached, as bishop, at a visitation. It was practical advice given directly to parish clergy. There are hundreds of these charges and sermons, delivered at ordinations and visitations. Reading them, you soon notice that the bar is not always set as high as Chrysostom had it.

So, for example, Gilbert Burnet, Bishop of Salisbury, could quote with approval the work of Nazianzus, Chrysostom and

Gregory the Great, but his own guidance to the clergy had a more jaundiced tone. A historian, he believed that the record showed that the protestant clergy

> fell from their First Heat and Love; they began to build Houses for themselves, and their Families, and neglected the House of God: They rested satisfied with their having reformed the Doctrine and Worship; but did not study to reform the Lives and Manners of their People.[7]

Burnet thought that vocation could fail and be replaced with a terrible empty performance. He suspected that the clergy had inoculated themselves against the alarming truths they handled by resorting to dull routine: 'a stupid Formality, and a Callus that he Contracts, by his insensible way of handling Divine Matters; by which he becomes hardened against them'.[8]

Gilbert Burnet was an extraordinary character; the chaste and disciplined prose of the *Dictionary of National Biography* strains every fibre to contain him and ultimately labels him an 'egomaniac'. His career lurched from crisis to crisis as his irrepressible talent and opinion first attracted and then repelled successive monarchs and aristocrats. He found great patrons and then he offended them; it was the only thing he ever did consistently. Even at the point he was made Bishop of Salisbury, in 1689, the King was observing that he was a 'wretched Tartuffe'. Here was a man who could write with authority about unpopularity and criticism. Few clergy have courted disapproval as thoroughly as did Burnet, but he has something important to say in recognizing that the clergy must expect criticism; it should neither surprise, nor annoy them. The real threat in Burnet's eyes was the temptation to respond in kind:

> a haughty and huffing humour, an impatient and insolent temper, a loftiness of deportment and a peevishness of spirit, rendering the lives of the clergy, for the most part, bitter to themselves … A clergyman must be prepared to bear injuries, to endure much unjust censure and calumny, to see himself often neglected, and others preferred to him, in the esteem of

the People. He that takes all this ill, that resents it, and complains of it, does thereby give himself much disquiet, and to be sure, he will, through his Peevishness, rather increase than lessen that Contempt, under which he is so uneasy.[9]

In the seventeenth and eighteenth centuries anxiety about the behaviour and commitment of the clergy was commonplace. These were not great days for the ordained ministry. There were, of course, any number of dedicated and even exceptional priests, but there were others who impressed less, and John Wesley was near to despair about the casual attitude taken to vocation:

> Alas, what terrible effects do we continually see of that common though senseless imagination, 'The boy, if he is fit for nothing else, will do well enough for a Parson!' Hence it is, that we see (I would to God there were no such instance in all Great Britain, or Ireland!) dull, heavy, blockish Ministers; men of no life, no spirit, no readiness of thought.[10]

Routinely, bishops set the nature of the calling before their clergy, urged them to read over their ordination vows and reminded them of the promises they had made.[11] It is a technique we use still; development review meetings with an archdeacon or an area dean are often arranged round phrases lifted from the ordination service. It is grounded in the assumption that we might forget the promises we made.

Pirate kings

Ministry is a privilege; it can be joyful; it is tough. It is no more difficult for the clergy to work out their vocation than it is for anyone else. The particular challenge the clergy face is simply that expectation is so high and failure so public. Indeed, we find the clergy and the possibility of failure so fascinating that it becomes the stuff of fiction, whether they are hypocrites like Arthur Dimmesdale, or just flawed, like the unnamed priest in *The Power and the Glory*.[12] We have always known it is a privilege and we have always known it is tough. We have been good at the aspiration. All the authors mentioned here have been very good indeed at the aspiration. We have been less good at writing about falling short of the aspiration. Bishops' charges engage with the reality of clergy who disappoint by sounding warnings and providing rules. Recent authors, who have begun to talk more and more openly about the difficulty and challenge of ministry, offer advice on well-being, sleep and time-off.[13] Those are things that will help with the symptoms of failure.

What wisdom can we summon up when failure stares us in the face? Rescued all those years ago by my bishop, I have been rescued again and again by the holiness of some priests and the sanity and humour of others; I have been sustained by the kindness and prayers of the communities around me. I have, I notice, also been held on course by the routines I have to live by. I have been rescued, in short, by the Church. It is, as we have seen, peculiarly the job of the clergy to help us find our place within the Church. It is the point made by Lightfoot, that the clergy do not make the Church, they are made by it. However high we make our doctrine of priesthood, our doctrine of the Church must be higher. Worried about my responsibilities, I have too often forgotten that I am being sustained too. It was only when my father died and I had to accept the ministry of colleagues and the affection of the congregation that I really noticed what had been there all along.

The contemporary insistence on leadership and a significant step change in the determination to provide proper training has equipped a lot of us better for the task. We are more focused on context. We are newly serious about the scale of the challenge. Ministry is refreshed and we are appropriately equipped to say something in this generation. These new assumptions are needed, but they can shoulder out the language of love that is supposed to be at the heart of the Church. As we narrow our eyes and put on a new determination, we face new temptations to take ourselves too seriously and to make ourselves the main event. Outcomes and strategic goals are useful tools, but purpose sometimes forces out patience and we never write poetry around these goals. We need reminding, constantly, that we are held in the same community in which we try to include others.

I had a wise and wily spiritual director for a few years (he died far too soon). He told me, more than once, that the problem for most clergy was that they were struggling to be saints when their natural disposition was to become a pirate king. It was an important lesson that he was trying to teach me and it worked on a number of levels. He was telling me, as Director of Ministry, not to be so surprised that the leaders did not always want to be led. He was telling me that there was more than a bit of the pirate king in me and to watch that. And he was reminding me, gently, that salvation comes to us in church in the city of God, the Kingdom of God, in the body of Christ. Salvation is always for us all, it is not set aside for the people who cast themselves as heroes.

Keeping it simple

How do we see off the pirate king? How do we remind ourselves that we belong to the community too? It is the reason we have spiritual directors and confessors, it is the reason we think chapters, cell groups and prayer partners matter. Lightfoot was right, we need also to rely on the routines of the Church. Just getting on with the job is sometimes the best way to both understand it and survive it. Lightfoot relied on that solution during one crisis of identity for the clergy. In the thirteenth century, in the middle of another such crisis, a similar solution was offered. With the arrival of the friars a new insistence on confession and spiritual counsel swept through the Church, demanding new skills. A string of penitential manuals appeared and simply urged the clergy to attend to some very basic disciplines. These books provided a 'back to basics' approach, an insistence on simple things, confident perhaps that God in his grace would do the rest. Here is John Mirk on the challenge of listening to a woman's confession:

Stylle as ston ther thow sytte,
And kepe the welle that thou ne spytte
Koghe thow not thenne, thy thonkes,
Ny wrynge thou not with thy schonkes,
Lest heo suppose thow make that fare,
For wlatynge that thou herest thare.

sit still as stone
be disciplined, don't spit
don't cough, don't show your thoughts
Nor cross your legs
lest she suppose you make this fuss
for loathing of what you hear.[14]

The penitential manuals knew the scope and scale of the calling
and kept it simple:

A preste owe to be holy, deperted or disseuerede fro synnes,
a gouernour and not a rauenour, a true stuard or dispensour
and not a wastour, piteous in doome, rightful in consel, true
in worde, meke in company, paciente in aduersite, benynge
and mylde in prosperite, rych in virtues, a knight stronge in
gu dedes, sobure in quere, chaste in herte, wyse in confession,
sekyr in prechynge.[15]

Live with the promise of salvation and the possibilities of
sin. Live with that promise and then turn down the volume
a little. It is too easy to take ourselves and our vocation too
seriously. Too much moody reflection on the drama of it will
make cowards of us all. We need to know the seriousness of
the task and then we need to get on with it, attending to the
little things. Knowing why we do it, we concentrate on how to
do it, because the how matters. John Drury made the point in
a Lent Book in 1990:

I may be saying something plausible or officially correct, but
if I blush and fidget, or if my voice gets hesitant or shrill, I
give away more truth than I would like ... Manner matters.

St Paul put it definitively in the thirteenth chapter of his first
letter to the Corinthians: whatever we do is empty if it is not
done in the way and manner of love ... Interest in what [reli-
gious people] do at church and how they do it, is as valid as
interest in what they say there. When people going out of
church thank the vicar for taking the service nicely they are
making a fundamental point.[16]

The same point was made by Thomas Hall: 'See to the manner of
your Thanksgiving, God loves Adverbs better than Adjectives.'[17]

Know why you do it. Know why you do it above all else
and then concentrate on the adverbs, do it graciously, do it
thankfully, do it prayerfully. Not what you do, but how you
do it. It is an idea wonderfully captured by Paul Durcan in the
poem 'The 12 O'Clock Mass, Roundstone, County Galway, 28
July 2002'. There, a priest entirely at home in himself and in
his mammoth trainers presides at a Eucharist that is full of fun
and affection and holiness. It is a long poem with a memorable
exchanging of the Peace and a prayer for a game of hurling.
It has the priest dismiss the congregation with an instruction
to enjoy themselves, 'that is what God made you to do'; read
it. It is the job of every priest to remind us of the staggering
extravagance of grace and then make that grace and priesthood
ordinary.

Deadness and flatness

In the mid-seventeenth century clergy and others routinely kept
diaries and practised a form of recollection. It was a time when
a desire to seek out the signs of salvation fostered a powerfully
introspective spirituality. John Janeway, ordained and a fellow
of King's College, Cambridge, spent nearly all of his time at his
books, but each evening set that study aside and took stock of
himself:

What incomes and profit he received in his spiritual traffique;
what returns from that far country; what answers of prayer,

what deadness and flatness, and what observable providences did present themselves ... this brought him a very intimate acquaintance with his own heart.[18]

'Deadness and flatness' are what he found and he lived with it. They are part, a very familiar part, of the experience of ministry. I am no kind of expert, but I think the only other point that must be made about living with the possibility of failure in ministry is that we must accept that we will fail. We were always going to fail and we will go on failing again and again. Christ called his disciples and warned them that the world would hate them, they were never going to fit in. Christ came to reveal the life and love of God and showed us that it looked like dying rejected and abused. Christian vocation is always a vocation to fail, and the vocation to ministry is just the same vocation to fail while standing facing the congregation.

I started with the great texts on ministry, the prose of Gregory, Ambrose, Baxter and Liddon. My argument here has been that we know more than we have sometimes remembered about the life and work of a priest, about ministry, lay and ordained. We have a shared calling to live the life of Christ. We also have the riches of sustained reflection on why public holiness might matter, why it is important to hold richness and variety in communion, why theology matters, why we need words for the Kingdom in a parish. It is my belief there is not just wisdom in these texts, but a confidence in what a calling into ministry looks like when it is being worked out. I suggest that we can find here a bracing reminder that ministry is not a possession, a simple task, a single focus.

Each of us works out ministry for ourselves. Ministry is various and more unstable than we would like. The summons can be clear, but the life that follows does not advance in a straight line. It is the poets who seem to express that truth most clearly. R. S. Thomas summed up for many of us the bleakest of the challenges in ministry, 'vicar of large things'.[19]

You do it because you are called. We all do it because of that call; not because we will be good at it, but because we are under direction. It is harder now than it once was to use that language.

Appointments are based on careful job descriptions and lists of competencies (not much poetry there). Conversations about calling get swallowed up in discussions of skills, 'fit' and 'synergies'. Do we have time to examine what calling might mean when we are eager to establish strategic competence, financial literacy, management skills and achieve missional outcomes? Even so, we do it because we are called. God got hold of me and then his bishop would not let go that evening in Ely. We are called, it is a summons, we are called out of something, called into something radically more glorious than anything we can imagine, let alone adequately describe.

The greatest, and most familiar, of all the poems that wrestle with this calling is George Herbert's, 'The Collar'.

> I struck the board, and cried, No more;
>   I will abroad!
> What? shall I ever sigh and pine?

It is a headlong rush of complaint. It is startling in its angry energy, the board the poet strikes is a communion table. This priest really is dismayed. It is constraint that gets him down:

> My lines and life are free, free as the road,
> Loose as the wind, as large as store.
>   Shall I be still in suit?[20]

The collar is a kind of constraint, accept it and other possibilities have to be excluded; life acquires a particular direction. Summoned into the life of Christ, I will become fully human, but first I will have to master my desire to settle for less. My formation will be lifelong and it will not all be easy. You do it because it is worth doing; you do it because you are called.

George Herbert is contested ground. His critics find him outdated, and his guidance is often considered downright dangerous. Perhaps we really do know better now, and in our urgency to engage with a different context we need to put his and other books down. Or perhaps we have grown just a touch impatient and a little too fascinated by our own grim determination. The story is not about us, it was never just about us.

But as I raved and grew more fierce and wild
  At every word,
Methought I heard one calling, *Child!*
  And I replied *My Lord.*

Notes

1 J. Hall, *The Works of Joseph Hall … with some account of his life*, Oxford: Talboys, 1837–39, XI, p. 7.

2 Hall, *Works*, p. 17.

3 *Common Worship: Ordination Services*, London: Church House Publishing, 2007.

4 J. Taylor, *Rules and Advices to the Clergy, For their Deportment in their Personal and Publick Capacities*,1672, and reprinted in *The Clergyman's Instructor: or a Collection of Tracts on Ministerial Duties*, Oxford: 1843.

5 Taylor, *Rules and Advices*, II, pp. 96, 97.

6 Taylor, *Rules and Advices*, I, III, V, pp. 99, 104, 105.

7 G. Burnet, Preface to *Discourse of the Pastoral Care*, London: 1821, pp. xxviii, xxix.

8 Burnet, *Discourse of the Pastoral Care*, VII p. 159.

9 Burnet, *Discourse of the Pastoral Care*, VII p. 161.

10 J. Wesley, *Address to the Clergy*, in J. Wesley, *The Works of the Revd John Wesley, X*, London: John Mason, 1841, p. 470.

11 See S. Patrick, *The work of the Ministry Represented to the clergy of the Diocese of Ely*, London: J. J. F. & J. Rivington, 1841, p. 5, and T. Wilson, 'To the Clergy of the Diocese of Sodor and Man', reprinted in *The Clergyman's Instructor, or A Collection of Tracts on the Ministerial Duties*, Oxford: Oxford University Press, 1843, p. 377.

12 Dimmesdale features in Nathaniel Hawthorne's *The Scarlet Letter*, Boston, MA: 1850.

13 J. Lewis-Anthony, *If You Meet George Herbert on the Road, Kill Him: Radically Re-Thinking Priestly Ministry*, London: Mowbray; M. Dudley and V. Rounding, *The Parish Survival Guide*, London: SPCK, 2004; G. Oliver, *Ministry without Madness*, London: SPCK, 2012.

14 J. Mirk, *Instructions for Parish Priests*, ed. E. Peacock, London: Early English Text Society, 1848, p. 24, line 777. Available online: https://archive.org/details/instructionsforoofurngoog.

15 G. Holmstedt (ed.), *Speculum Christiani*, Early English Text Society, vol. 182, London: Oxford University Press, 1933, p. 230.

16 J. Drury, *The Burning Bush*, London: Collins, 1990, p. 13.

17 T. Hall, *A practical and polemical commentary: or, exposition*

upon the third and fourth chapters of the latter epistle of Saint Paul to Timothy, London: 1658, p. 71.

18 James Janeway, *Invisible Realities, Demonstrated in the Holy Life and Triumphant Death of Mr John Janeway*, Glasgow: John Bryce, 1772, p. 59.

19 R. S. Thomas, from *The Echoes Return Slow*, London: Macmillan, 1988.

20 G. Herbert, 'The Collar', from *The Temple*, in F. E. Hutchinson (ed.), *The Works of George Herbert*, Oxford: Oxford University Press, 1941.

Index of Biblical References

Exodus
3:1ff   113
16:3   60–61

Leviticus
19:18   133

Numbers
17   136

Psalms
19:1   30
148:7–10   139

Isaiah
6:5   113
60:17   136

Jeremiah
1:6   5

Matthew
12:40   50
13:31   37
13:44   55
13:55   62
20:1   55
21:23   61
21:33   132

Mark
1:22   61
10:37   106

Luke
4:36   61
5:8   113
10:25ff.   158
12:35–46   147
22:26   76

John
10:41   110
17:1–2   61
17:22   38
21:18   106
21:20–21   121

Acts
2:6   55
20:28   124

Romans
12:6   132

I Corinthians
1:17   142
2:2   142
3:9   37, 132
11:26   142
12:4   175
12:4–10   132
12:28   64

Ephesians
1:22   132
4:11–13   140
4:13   134
5:25   132, 142
6:12   119

Colossians
1:18   132
1:21–22   142

I Timothy
3:4–5   71

Titus
1:8   71

Hebrews
7:25   146–147
13:17   42

I Peter
2:5   49
2:9   132

I John
1:3   37
3:2   142

Revelation
14:2   55
19:9   37
21:2   37, 132

Index of Names

Allen, Roland 70–72, 84
Ambrose, bishop of Milan 29, 153–158, 161, 162, 172, 185
Aquinas, Thomas 88
Arsenius, Abba 88
Augustine, bishop of Hippo 29, 77, 153
Austen, Jane 101

Baxter, Richard 4, 97, 122–128, 176, 177, 178, 185
Blunt, John James 107
Bonhoeffer, Dietrich 3
Bridger, Francis 33
Burnet, Gilbert 178–180

Carr, Wesley 13, 21–28, 32, 33, 34, 105
Chadwick, Henry 37
Chaucer, Geoffrey 101
Cicero 155
Clement of Alexandria 30, 84
Clement of Rome 75, 113, 118, 134–141, 135, 148, 151
Clifford, Lady Anne 92
Chrysostom, John 91, 117–121, 122, 125, 126, 176, 178
Clitherow, Andrew 156
Croft, Steven 11
Cyprian, bishop of Carthage 47–51, 113, 140

Daniel 56
Denny, Thomas 139

Didache 63–66, 67, 69, 71, 72, 75, 76, 78, 84, 85, 98, 105, 118, 132, 134, 136
Dickinson, Emily 121
Dillard, Annie 159
Drury, John 183
Duffy, Eamon xi, 16, 72
Durcan, Paul 184

Edmondson, Chris 11
Elijah 103, 159
Ezekiel 56

Fabian, bishop of Rome 48
Fife, Janet 80
Fisher, Geoffrey 141
Fisher, John 28–31, 32, 33, 34

Garrigou-Lagrange, Reginald 122
Green Report 14, 15, 33
Gore, Charles 67–70, 84, 136
Greenwood, Robin 11, 72–78, 84, 98
Gregory I (the Great) 28, 153, 158–166, 172, 179, 185
Guidelines for Professional Conduct 12, 20, 32

Hall, Joseph 175, 176
Hall, Thomas 184
Herbert, Edward 89
Herbert, George 47, 88–98, 115, 122, 123, 178, 186, 187